PORCUPINES AT THE DANCE

Parables and Stories from Colliding Rivers

MICHAEL HARRINGTON

Susan Creek Books
Wilsonville, Oregon

PORCUPINES AT THE DANCE

Parables and Stories from Colliding Rivers

Copyright 2008 Michael Harrington
First Edition — 2008

Cover design and illustration by Brenda Evans
Initial edit by Judith Irwin
Final edit by Karla Joy McMechan
Typesetting by Brenda Evans
Proofread by Deanna Riebe

ISBN #: 978-0-9748716-1-5
Library of Congress #: 2007942362

Susan Creek Books
29030 SW Town Center Loop E.
Suite 202-250
Wilsonville, OR 97070
(503) 516-1106
www.SusanCreek.com

Printed in the United States by Morris Publishing
3212 East Highway 30
Kearney, NE 68847
1-800-650-7888

DEDICATION

To the holder of the Golden Heart

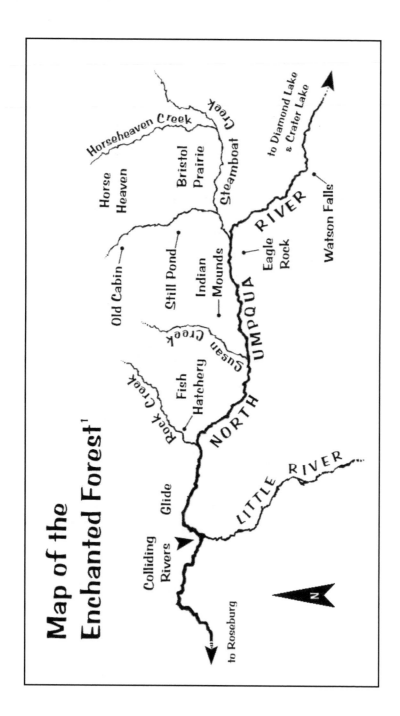

Map of the Enchanted Forest[1]

TABLE OF CONTENTS

NOTE: Conversations with John Redstone appear in **Bold** type in this table, parables in "Regular" type, and poems in *Italics*.

AUTHOR'S NOTE

My purpose in writing the Colliding Rivers series has been to record the conversations I had with a great Soul, a man I called John Redstone in *Touched by the Dragon's Breath: Conversations at Colliding Rivers.*[2] Prior to his translation from this life in 2001, my friend gave me his written permission to pass along his wealth of self-knowledge. To protect the privacy of his living relatives, I have fictionalized names and places where I deemed necessary; but in all cases I have done my best to preserve the integrity of his ideas.

In my own life, between the ages of seventeen and twenty-one, a great spiritual unrest was brewing. I rebelled against conventional religion, grew my hair long (as an expression of my dissatisfaction), and, following the lead of my dreams, began studying metaphysics.

One day, amid this transition, a surprising thing happened—I wrote two dozen parables in a twenty day span. "Channeled" might be a better term, for they seemed to come out of thin air. I was living in a tent at the time, and hiking during the day in the Colliding Rivers area near Glide, Oregon.

Upon meeting Mr. Redstone, a man who shared my appreciation for the trails and backroads of Oregon, many things fell into place. For one, when I began recording our conversations, I discovered an uncanny link between these spiritual discussions and my small collection of parables. In fact, they fit together hand in glove!

The merging of these two seemingly independent writings began as a semi-fictional work, loosely based on my initial meetings and conversations with my friend and mentor. It soon became apparent, however, that a remarkable inner journey was taking shape. As I took these conversations and stories into contemplation during the writing process, the book began to take on a life all its own. An intriguing subplot developed. I must admit, midway through, I was just as curious as any reader to find out what Mr. Redstone would discover upon his return to the sacred valley of Horse Heaven, his spiritual home.

By the time *Porcupines at the Dance* was finished, one of the reasons Mr. Redstone had come into my life had become clear. I also understood why the ending moved me as it did. Something else piqued my interest. Throughout the book I found subtle clues that pointed indirectly to the origin of the parables.

More recent contemplations have revealed past life images from various Native American settings. As stated in *Dragon's Breath,* I first began calling Mr. Redstone "the Chief" when talking about him with friends. It may have sounded a bit flippant to some, but it felt right, so I continued. Perhaps the reference was a subconscious carryover from the past, I cannot say; but it was always meant as a gesture of respect.

Over the years I've met many remarkable people, but none more memorable than John Redstone. He was an intelligent, well-traveled individual, who always returned to the mountains of Oregon. What my friend lacked in material wealth and social position, he made up for in personal freedom and integrity.

Today I can better appreciate the spiritual lessons the Chief wanted to pass along. Come share the wisdom one man discovered in the Enchanted Forest that was his life.

> – Michael Harrington
> Susan Creek, near Colliding Rivers
> July 2007

Chapter One
Truth

The Red Buffalo
CONVERSATION AT COLLIDING RIVERS

John Redstone gazed serenely into the mist above Colliding Rivers. He was tall, stately, kind —all the adjectives one might use to describe a benevolent grandfather. We had met only hours before, but I felt an immediate kinship with the amiable gentleman with the flowing grey hair who, as it turned out, was to be my traveling companion and teacher for the next several days. It wasn't long before we discovered a common interest in philosophy.

"Colliding Rivers has always been a special place to my people, the Umpquas," he said, taking a seat beside me on a rough-hewn bench. Of the six bands indigenous to southern Oregon, my ancestors, the *Nezic,* lived the closest to Colliding Rivers.[3]

"My grandfather believed that the merging of the North Umpqua and Little River was a symbol for truth. He came here when he needed answers or inspiration. Sometimes he would bring me here fishing. He used to call me *Young Heron.*" Mr. Redstone smiled at the memory. "He said it was because I was such a good fisherman. I missed him a lot when he died, especially his stories. I was only eight."

A logging truck roared past on the North Umpqua highway, throwing up a rooster tail of dust. In its wake, a car with California plates turned into the parking lot.

"Many of the sight-seers that pull in at the Colliding Rivers viewpoint can sense something magical, too," he continued. "They stop to read the plaque, then lean over the wooden railing and stare into the mist for awhile before moving on to Crater Lake. They never realize how close they've been to the Almighty," he remarked. "The Great Spirit was gazing back at them from beyond the mist of duality." Mr. Redstone glanced over to see how I had reacted to his reference to God before continuing.

"When I was in my early twenties I did a lot of traveling. I had a great desire to find the answers to life, and college wasn't as important as it is today. When I heard that India was a popular spiritual destination I hopped a ship bound for Bombay, then took a train to the foothills of the Himalayas. A famous teacher known as the 'Great Master' had an ashram, or retreat, there.

"He was rather tall by East Indian standards, with translucent skin that radiated a healthy glow. Generally he wore a simple white robe and turban, not wanting to set himself above others in any way. He was the embodiment of kindness and compassion.

"When I showed up on his doorstep, I announced with youthful enthusiasm that I'd come to India to find God. He laughed good-naturedly, and then told me that I could have saved myself a lot of trouble. He said that since God was everywhere, He was just as much in America as He was in India. But he offered to let me stay for a few days before going home.

"Well, days turned into weeks, then weeks to months. All in all, I spent close to two years at his ashram. It was there that I found a skill for growing herbs and vegetables...and in the end I did learn a great deal from this master, including where God really is."

I'd heard stories about India and Tibet, and like my new friend, the man I affectionately called "the Chief," I had been harboring the same age-old question about the location of the Creator. Since the age of fourteen, I'd felt a need to look for God outside of organized religion. The Chief could tell that he had my attention.

"I learned that although God is present everywhere and in everything," he continued, "His face can never be seen in this world; not in the grandeur of a Himalayan sunrise, not in the beauty of a South Pacific sunset.

"You see, God is the Infinite Ocean of Love resting within Itself. To use a metaphor, God is like a great white wall. We can draw anything on the wall we can imagine, for it contains everything, right? Let's say we take a red crayon and draw the picture of a buffalo." The Chief made a sweeping motion in the air as he spoke. "It might be easier for you to visualize if you close your eyes and use your imagination," he suggested.

"The red buffalo has only become recognizable because it has separated itself from the All and

Nothing of the wall, Divine Unity. But something else has emerged, as well. You see, the red buffalo was not allowed to leave Divine Unity on his journey into form alone. If we could see the other side of the wall we would find his female traveling companion, a green buffalo! The entire visible world is only half of a perfectly matched whole."

The Chief explained further. "The white wall is perfectly still. It is motionless. This is why our senses can't detect it, even though it is present everywhere. Now, this gets a bit complicated. From His realm of Infinite Bliss and Eternal Stillness, God images the *idea* of creation. Everything that has ever existed, or that ever will exist, is contained in God's dream of creation. For this reason, creation is finished. This archetypal idea exists as a hologram of light.

"It isn't possible to take a single idea and separate it from the whole. It is necessary to take a picture of the idea, so to speak. This picture can then be split into two complementary halves, like the red and the green buffalo. But understand: Only the idea is real. The simulated picture is not the idea it represents. What our senses tell us is real is but the shadow of reality, a cosmic, three-dimensional motion picture.

"In order to experience motion it is necessary to form a polarity. This is why the red buffalo could not make the journey into form by himself. When a polarity is formed, an exchange of energy is possible. This energy exchange takes place within each light wave in the universe. To understand this *Rhythmic Balanced Interchange* between opposites within the light wave is to understand creation!

"When we detect motion in the expressive phase of creation, we say something is 'alive.' When opposites return to stillness in the voidance phase, the pulse of life ceases. With our limited understanding of God's cycles of motion and rest, the two phases of creation, we say that it is 'dead.' This expression of ideas, and their subsequent return to stillness, is sometimes called the *Outbreath* and *Inbreath* of God."

The Chief paused to let the new ideas sink in. He had a simple way of explaining difficult concepts. It was something I grew to appreciate more and more after entering college. The scent of sweet buttercups drifted toward us on a northwest breeze. It brought to mind a twilight walk with a new girlfriend through a field of daisies and wild strawberries up Little River.

That summer evening I'd been touched by a sacredness I'd never found in church. No minister had ever mentioned the Infinite Ocean of God's Love, either. Remembering the many Sundays and Wednesday nights I'd squirmed through sermons about a wrathful god and eternal damnation brought up an unexpected surge of anger. The Chief's calm voice brought me back to the present.

"Everything seeks God, because God is the center of everything. It is the one true reality, the 'Unchanging Ocean of Ecstasy.' For this reason, we must always go within to find truth. We must center our attention at the spiritual eye with the desire to know God.

"Consciousness arises from the desire To Be. This energy of desire is the energy of creation. It has but one purpose — to create an effect. When an idea is split into opposites and is set into motion in a light wave, the energy of desire is also divided. We experience this energy in motion as 'E-motion.'

"Few people realize the great power of imagination. It is more than the fantasy of little children. It is a direct line to the whole of life. By using the imagination to put our desires into picture form, we bypass the limitations of the lower mind and tap into God's great reservoir of ideas. When we use the imagination to establish self-knowledge, our own truth, then we won't have to depend on textbooks, which are really only the beliefs and opinions of others."

Mr. Redstone threw a pebble over the rock wall, then continued in an introspective tone. "Truth, like love, is infinite in nature, boundless by design. It encompasses all life and, like the imagination, is only limited by our inability to see the big picture.

"God has given us His greatest gift, the gift of choice," the Chief explained. "But most people choose shallow and unproductive lives. They find it easiest to live off the opinions of others. They choose to spend their time arguing over the outward shadows of reality. Of those who desire the great truth of God, only a few will have the childlike wonder necessary to find it. Fewer still will have the courage needed to surrender to its infinite power.

"But that's okay," the Chief said gently. "In time man always returns to truth, no matter how far he may wander. It is his destiny." He turned and looked directly at me. The bright brown eyes held a strange familiarity. "This is why we have come to Colliding Rivers," my young friend," he said. "The Infinite has beckoned us."

*   *   *

That night after dinner the Chief built a crackling fire near the water's edge. It was a ritual he repeated most evenings on our weeklong trek up the Umpqua. During this quiet time we reflected on our daily discussions. To further illuminate points made during the day, the Chief shared parables and stories relating to the subject. Many he attributed to his grandfather.

In each chapter I've included these stories (along with mine) in the pages immediately following the day's discourse. The first night's tales augmented our earlier conversation at Colliding Rivers, man's search for truth.

Where Rivers Collide

Two rivers run through the Enchanted Forest: the mighty North Umpqua and gentle Little River. The Umpqua is swift and surprising in power.[4] Its shoreline is rocky. It winds its way between towering cliffs. Little River flows with a quiet grace through bountiful orchards and lush green meadows. Children play on its sandy beaches.

Both rivers are blessed with the same rare fish, but their differences are striking. The fish of the Umpqua have red eyes, while the eyes of those in Little River are emerald green. The red-eyed fish are spirited and aggressive. They swim alone and exceedingly deep. The fish in Little River swim in groups near the tranquil surface. But unlike their brothers, they are passive by nature.

The Chief once made the acquaintance of an old fisherman with a long white beard. Together they would sit at Colliding Rivers. One stormy winter evening he told the Chief this story:

"When I was but a child," the old man began, "I met a skillful fisherman from a distant land. He had a mystery about him and a strange belief. He believed that ideas were not merely ideas. He believed they were the objects, themselves. Their physical counterparts, he claimed, were their three-dimensional shadows.

"He believed that these rare fish live in the minds of men, and that all the disharmony in the world could be traced to their differences. It was his belief that the union of the fish in our two rivers produce the truth that all men seek."

The old man sat rigidly, staring out into space, as if remembering something both wondrous and at the same time terrifying. "When the fisherman left me," the old man whispered hoarsely, "he cast no shadow, and the fish dangling from his belt gazed back at me with an eye that was red and an eye that was green."

The old man came out of his reverie and smiled. "There is a peacefulness here," he said; then almost as an afterthought added quietly, "in this place of power."

*   *   *

Few people fish where the rivers collide, for no one can be sure whether the old man casts his line out in wonder, or whether he casts it out in fear.

Opinions of Salmon

Two salmon returned from the ocean to the stream of their birth and swam beside a log where a muskrat and a hawk were sitting.

"How are things with the ocean?" asked the curious stream of the salmon. "As you know, streams become rivers, and rivers become oceans. I can hardly wait to experience the greatness I have heard so much about."

Said one salmon, "Greatness carries many burdens. And the burdens the ocean must carry are not like the small fishing boats the river bears. They are merchant ships, a thousand times longer than the length of a beaver."

"And the solitude," spoke the other salmon, "is beyond our ability to measure. Here you have other streams to converse with, but the ocean lives a solitary life indeed."

"In my opinion," advised the first, "I would remain a stream for as long as possible."

The stream was disturbed by the report, and immediately commissioned the beavers to construct a giant dam between itself and the river. For many seasons it remained a stream, content to live a life of ease. As time passed, however, weeds began to mar its beauty, for the life the stream had chosen was a shallow and unproductive life.

One autumn day after a very hot summer, the hawk returned to the same log and found the muskrat walking along a sun-baked creek bed. "What has become of our beautiful stream?" cried the surprised bird.

The muskrat shook his head sadly. "Our friend lived too long on the opinions of others."

Lifework

A muskrat read an in-depth treatise entitled *The Quest for Truth*, written by a prophet who lived in India. It took the muskrat over a year to read the thousand-page book, and when he had finished, he realized that he understood but little.

Leaving everything behind, the muskrat set off on a six-year journey that ended on the doorstep of his mentor, the prophet.

"I am only an ignorant muskrat," he said, "but I am a humble devotee of truth. It is my greatest dream to become a student of yours and learn firsthand what I failed to learn from your book."

The prophet surveyed the travel-worn muskrat a moment, then took pity upon him. "Perhaps we should start with what you have learned from my book," he said wisely.

"Oh benevolent teacher," the muskrat said with his head bowed low, "from all your great words I learned only this: If you love something enough it will give up its secret."

The prophet stared down at him in silence. At last he spoke. "I can teach you nothing," he said, then turned and quietly shut the door behind him. The stunned muskrat left for home in disappointment, thinking himself unworthy to be taught.

From an open window the prophet traced his footsteps. As the dejected muskrat stepped onto the footpath he overheard the prophet's cry of astonishment. "What an enlightened muskrat!" he marveled. "He said in one sentence what it took a lifetime for me to write."

Dance of the Hermit Porcupine

Two porcupines traveled a great distance to visit a friend from their youth, a porcupine who lived alone near the base of Eagle Rock. After reminiscing about old times, the conversation turned to philosophy.

"I have heard that Truth lives near the source of the Umpqua," said one of the visiting porcupines. "She is shy, some say, and her subtle beauty is seldom seen except by those who seek her devoutly."

"And I've heard that Truth lives along Little River," observed his traveling companion. "But she is not shy. She has many friends, and often plays with the children on the banks of the river."

The hermit porcupine gazed off into space, wondering if he should speak. At last he said quietly, "Truth, my dear friends, lives in the hearts of those who love it with all their Soul. It is neither male nor female, but is 'an infinite ocean of love and purity.'"

After he had spoken, the porcupine noticed troubled looks on the faces of his friends. "But let us not concern ourselves with such deep matters," he added wisely. "Let us dance."

As the three joined hands the hermit porcupine hummed a strange song, one his friends had never heard before. The two visiting porcupines glanced at one another, then smiled at their friend sadly, for although he was dancing with a new enthusiasm, his dancing was obviously out of step.

Boundless by Design

Should I be named the lord
of every field and woodlot I surveyed,
my freedom I would honor long before
one boundary I would make.

And should my choice extend
beyond the vistas human hands confine,
unto the distant stars, my voice would cry
for freedom undefined.

And even should the right
be granted me to pass through heaven's gate,
to occupy a land called free by some,
I still would hesitate.

But should I ever hear
of some fair kingdom boundless by design,
my freedom I would gladly lay aside
to call that parcel mine.

Chapter Two
Wisdom

The Secret Name of God
CONVERSATION AT ROCK CREEK

The next morning the Chief and I broke camp early. We walked in silence through a dense stand of old-growth timber, choosing to enjoy the beauty of the forest over conversation. Skittish deer, elk, bear, mountain lion, and a wide variety of smaller animals made their home here among the fir and pine.

The path we were following led back to the Umpqua, depositing us near the confluence of Rock Creek, known for its fish hatchery. We sat down on a log to rest and shared some trail mix. A summer steelhead, perhaps a newly released hatchery fish, broke the wind-blown surface of a pool fifty yards upstream. On the far side of the rippling river, a small, wooden fishing boat was tethered to an overhanging willow bough swaying in the wind. Years before I'd spent a weekend on Diamond Lake fishing from a similar craft with my father.

"Wisdom is a rare commodity in this world," stated the Chief, starting a discussion. "When we meet someone who has attained this spiritual gold, we will also find the light of love shining in his eyes.

"In fact, if we follow a path of wisdom, in the end there will always be love. By the same token, the path of love leads to wisdom. Hazrat Khan, the Sufi, taught that love and wisdom are in essence the same thing."[5] The cry of an osprey echoed off an adjacent hillside as if to emphasize the Chief's words.

"There are many ways to learn, as you are finding out. My grandfather taught me to study the animals. He said the mountain lion could teach me stealth, for instance, and the badger, tenacity. The otter loves to play. He is God's great ambassador of joy. My grandfather used to tell me that if I talked too much about trivial things, the Great Spirit would bring a jaybird around to show me how I sounded.

"We can also learn from our mistakes. When I was six," he confided, "I made friends with an old trapper who made a meager living dealing in beaver pelts. I used to steal away to his house whenever I could. He told colorful stories about savage mountain lions and dangerous grizzlies. Well, the man took a liking to me, and one day gave me a rusty trap. It changed my life, but not in the way you might imagine.

"One morning I got up early, before sunrise, and climbed a nearby hill. Very carefully I set the trap, then covered the opening with some dry grass to conceal it. My heart was pounding as I wheeled about for home, praying that I'd catch something worth talking about . . . and then fate intervened. I felt a pair of invisible hands push ever so slightly against my chest. I lost my balance and took a quick step back.

"I screamed in pain as the metal trap locked its powerful jaws around my ankle. For the first time, I thought about the animals. I learned what it felt like to be trapped. To make matters worse, I couldn't get out. I hobbled all the way home with the trap chewing the skin off my right ankle. My grandfather howled with laughter. I'd caught something worth talking about, all right. I was the center of unwanted attention and many jokes for quite sometime. I threw the trap away."

The Chief picked up a twig and tossed it into the swift current with a smile. Pointing across the river, he continued. "The willow teaches us about the Law of Non-Resistance. See how it bends with the wind? The heavy winter snow falls off the willow bough. On the other hand, the limbs of the mighty oak snap under the weight. You see, whenever we oppose anything in the universe we give it power.

"If we confront evil head-on we simply add to its strength. If we step out of the way, however, the destructive energy will find nothing to push against. It must go into the voidance phase of creation.

"Christ taught, 'Agree quickly with thine enemies.' Those who understand the Law of Non-Resistance have no interest in debating the issues of life. They quickly agree with those who wish to argue. Of course any argument is a comparison of apples and oranges anyway, since each person has his own *Belief System*.

"We generally think of wisdom as something to be gained. But wisdom also comes from eliminating outdated beliefs that give us false views of life.

Little do we know that when we make judgments about how things are, we are limiting our future possibilities. We are saying to ourselves, 'Every future event will be exactly like this one.'

"To give you an example, let's say that at the age of five we decide to climb the oak tree behind our house. What a great adventure. As fate would have it, however, we lose our grip and fall to the ground eight feet below, breaking our arm.

"From this painful experience we form a judgment: Climbing trees is dangerous. After that, whenever our friends climb trees to pick apples, cherries, or simply to enjoy the view, we wait for them at the bottom where it is safe.

"On top of that, when we reach adulthood and have kids of our own, we scream at them whenever they reach for a limb...because we *know* that climbing trees is dangerous. The truth of the matter is this: 'We fell from a tree once, got hurt, and have not yet released the fear.'

"Those beings we call masters have no such limitations hanging over their heads. They have cleaned out these limited snapshots of reality from the storage area in their reactive minds. They enjoy full knowledge of who they are and live life to its fullest. They even climb trees when they feel like it."

I asked the Chief how to remove these judgments from our Belief System. "It's very simple. **A higher understanding will automatically transmute a judgment of lower frequency.** We use our imagination to couch the experience in mental pictures. Mental pictures are more powerful than thoughts. We must also release any trapped emotional pain associated with the event.

"We can also learn from studying the lives of awakened masters," continued the Chief, "but we must always walk the path for ourselves. Some individuals will pretend to be masters. They hope to be looked upon as important spiritual authorities. This bolsters their ego. You might choose to practice discrimination in what you say around these people, for they tend to measure others by their own limitations. They will undermine your vision of reality if you let them. But even though their motives are selfish, you should never judge them too harshly or be overly critical. They are learning in a way that best suits their level of understanding.

"You can recognize authentic spiritual teachers by their willingness to serve all life with humility and compassion. Those adepts who teach beginning students on the path are no less qualified than their colleagues who instruct more advanced classes. Rather than teach from a book, they share what they know.

"Most importantly, they all have personal knowledge of the 'River of God,' sometimes called the 'Audible Lifestream.' It is also known as the 'Golden Thread,' because it weaves together all life in every realm of existence. It is a great wave of love flowing out of the center of all creation. It has created, and presently sustains, all life in every sphere. There is something very interesting about this energy, sometimes called Spirit, that is very important to anyone seeking the wisdom of God.

"Being of God, it is light; but it is also 'sound.' On each plane of creation it can be heard as a specific sound due to the different proportions of spirit mixed with matter. It flows from the fountainhead of God, downward and outward to the physical universe. It then returns once again to the center of all creation. Once we are aware of it, we can sit in silence and listen for its celestial strains. When Soul hears this music it yearns to go home, although at this point it doesn't remember where home is.

"Those rare adepts who have traced this 'Music of the Spheres' to Its source all say that in the highest heavens the various sounds meld into one, the sound of *HU* (pronounced HYOO). This is the secret name of the Divine Being. It is a sacred repetition that opens the heart to love."[6]

Mr. Redstone cleared his throat and continued. "Do you remember how I described God as the Infinite Ocean of Love?" I nodded my head. "It's impossible for an Infinite Being to experience things of a finite nature, like going for a walk along Little River. For this reason, God must limit Itself. It must isolate a drop from the Ocean, so to speak, in order to experience ideas in motion.

"*We* are these individualized drops of God's love, here to further His quest for Self-discovery. Only through man's eyes does God experience still ideas in motion. Motion is necessary, because without it there can be no physical experience. God came up with a wonderful tool that could be used to divide His ideas into opposites on the polarity shaft of a light wave. It's called a mind.

"In the true realm of God — sometimes called 'All That Is'— there is infinite light. The material worlds, however, are comprised of simulated light, or light waves. This reflection of All That Is could be called 'All That Is Not, But Appears To Be.'

"All light waves are cube-shaped vacuum chambers bounded by inert gasses. The concept for television came from the light wave of creation. The Golden Thread connects each light wave to every other light wave in the universe at the still point of mind in the center, the fulcrum. This vast communication network coordinates all activities in the universe.

"God, as Creator, stands beyond the mist of duality in the realm of Pure Being. Therefore, we cannot know God with the mind, His tool for creating the worlds of experience. Thinking about God can't bring us closer to Him. How does this relate to wisdom? We can only know God by moving from thinking into knowing, and finally into being. Wisdom is a quality of God. We can only *be* God!"

The Chief rose from the log and brushed himself off. A startled chipmunk darted across the path before us and disappeared into a huckleberry thicket.

"If we walk with love," he observed, "we need never walk alone again, for wisdom will be our companion into the heart of God."

The Lights in the Sky

One clear night the animals met to discuss the lights in the sky. At length, an eagle was chosen to make the long journey and report back to the others on what he had found. Courageously, he flew deep into space, splashing stars aside with his powerful wings. Soon, he was lost in the splendor of a million suns.

From out of the ethers came an unspeakable sound that struck the eagle dumbfounded. "Welcome, Beloved One, to the Land Beyond the Sky. The lights you see about you are my infinite suns. Around them spin worlds much like your own, in numbers exceeding your ability to count. Because of your courage, I appoint you as my messenger to planet Earth, where your forest is hardly more than a speck of dust. Return and tell the others the truth about the things you have seen. Tell them of my love for every creature."

The eagle flew home bursting with excitement. "Good friends of the forest," he proclaimed, "I bring you great news. The lights in the sky are gigantic suns, each supporting countless worlds like our own. These planets are more numerous than the trees in the Enchanted Forest. Each world is blessed by the One, Great Creator with myriad life forms; yet His love for each of us is immeasurable. Indeed, a grain of sand along the bank of the Umpqua is more significant than the place our world occupies in the Land Beyond the Sky."

The animals turned their backs to the eagle and talked among themselves. "We should have sent the owl," whispered the bear. "The eagle has been blinded by his own limitations." One by one the creatures of the forest expressed their disappointment. At last, the eagle flew off by himself to contemplate upon what had happened.

The next night he returned with his head bowed low. "Please forgive me," he pleaded. "Last night I was moonstruck; but tonight my memory is clear. The truth, my good friends, is as you suspected. The lights in the sky are the eyes of the gods, all focused upon our Enchanted Forest."

When he had finished, the crowd exploded in applause. "I knew he'd come through!" shouted the bear. In memory of the occasion, a statue was raised and dedicated to the eagle as a tribute to his great courage and wisdom.

Winter of the Prophet

One summer a poet moved far into the woods seeking inspiration from nature. He built a small cabin, then spent his days wandering silently among the animals, waiting for the words of truth and beauty to return.

Autumn arrived with its colorful leaves and harvest moon, but still no inspiration came. At last, one winter day, the dejected poet faced the inevitable. It was time to return to the city and take a menial job for sustenance. Wearily, he cast one last glance heavenward and cried out, "My God, my God, why hast thou forsaken me?"

As if in answer to his plea, a single snowflake fell from the clear sky and landed on the poet's nose. An inner dam broke, and a flood of inspiration poured from his lips. The surprised animals were captivated by the poet's words.

Snow fell for three days and nights as the multitude was uplifted by great and noble truths cast in sublime images of poetic beauty. Each walked away feeling fortunate to have been present at the monumental event. The bear was even awakened from his winter's nap so that he could be privy to the illuminated truths while they were still fresh in everyone's mind.

But as the great bear lumbered from his den, he was greeted by an unusual sight. Many of the animals were walking about with their noses held high in the air, hoping to catch a snowflake sent from God. The belief spread quickly, for everyone wanted to be recognized as a great prophet. Only the bear laughed at the foolishness and refused to walk in such an arrogant manner… and the falcon, whose laughter was a jealous laughter.

To everyone's surprise, a blue jay was the first to catch a snowflake on his nose. A crowd soon gathered at the jaybird's feet, wondering what poetic truths would fall upon their hungry Souls like manna from heaven. For hours on end, the animals sat before the chattering jay awaiting the first crumb of wisdom.

Sadly, as the sun was setting on the third day, many lost faith and started for home in bitterness and disappointment. Even the patient badgers finally gave up hope. Only the jay was happy, for it was the first time in his life that anyone had willingly listened to anything he had to say.

"It was just as I suspected," cried the falcon. "There was no truth in what the prophet said. The lesser creatures of the forest were easily fooled, but not me."

Finally, the bear, seeing that sanity had been restored, returned to his simple dreams and slept more deeply than usual knowing the truth about snowflakes sent from God.

Two Kinds of Travelers

A man of vast formal education stopped by the cabin of the poet-prophet and introduced himself with a charismatic smile. When he noticed the crowd that had gathered to hear the prophet's words, he brought up his own extensive background on matters of philosophy. For many years he had been a student of Kant, Nietzsche, Schopenhauer, and many others too numerous to name. The stranger asked the prophet if he would care to debate the issues of life sometime. But the prophet politely declined.

After the man had gone the animals turned searching looks upon their simple teacher. Why, they wondered, had he backed down from the debate? Was the knowledge of the stranger superior to that of the prophet, who had never mentioned a single one of the great minds under which the scholar had studied?

The prophet understood their concern and spoke. "There are many paths through the forest, as you know," he said, "but only two kinds of travelers—those who walk with love, and those who don't."

The Old Road

An old road once ran through the Enchanted Forest. Its fame was such that many believed the entire Earth was spanned by its length. Only a few travelers passed through the forest in those days, however, and eventually the passage was swallowed up by the wild rose and blackberry. But to those who lived during that day and time, the road was a subject of much controversy.

Some believed the old road had been constructed by an ancient race of men, swept from the face of the Earth by the great flood. Others speculated that it had been created at the beginning of time, and that the forest had grown up around it. Some believed the great road had its point of origin in the Enchanted Forest; then there were some who argued that the forest marked its ending. But those days are gone now, and only a few are left who can still remember the old road.

Sometimes the old ones sit around the park and laugh about the great controversy surrounding the old road. Yes, they were happy days indeed, they all agree. But some of the old-timers swear the road ran north and south, while others argue that it ran east to west.

Builders of Boats

On Sunday afternoons the prophet often invited some of the animals to join him on his journeys up Little River. One day, to his surprise, two muskrats who had long been loyal passengers approached him with news of their discontent.

In a far-off land on the edge of a jungle, or so they had heard, lived another prophet, one who had built a wondrous boat. The river he crossed was much greater than tiny Little River.

"Go then," the prophet urged them, "and find your happiness. Seek out this great builder of boats."

When at last the two muskrats arrived at their destination, they found the stories to be true. The prophet of the jungle stood at the helm of a massive boat, heavily loaded with hippos and rhinoceros. As the muskrats approached him, they looked out in awe across the swift and dangerous crocodile-filled river.

"We have heard of your fame," they said timidly, "as a great builder of boats. We have left the prophet of the forest in order to ride with you on your great journeys."

The jungle prophet studied the tiny muskrats with a frown. "It is true," he finally said. "I am a great builder of boats. But so is the prophet of the forest. In fact, the boats we build are built equally well. You must understand, a master boat builder obeys the Law of Economy. He builds only to fit his needs. It would be as foolish for the prophet of the forest to build a boat to carry tigers as it would be for me to build a muskrat-sized boat. But since you are here, come aboard and take a seat beside the elephants."

A terrible fear swept through the hearts of the tiny muskrats as they gazed up at the clumsy elephants. They trembled involuntarily as the feeding calls of lions drifted from the opposite shore. The prophet, seeing the fear riveting them to where they stood, laughed a booming laugh.

"Go back to your forest," he advised. "Go back to your safe little river and your muskrat-sized boat. But go back knowing that your prophet's fame as a great builder of boats is known even here in the jungle. When you have outgrown the forest and your belly is the size of a hippo's, come back and ride with me!"

River of God

Onward ever
singing river,
flowing on forever free.
Life that fills us,
charms and thrills us,
draws its light and love from Thee.

Ascending, falling,
softly calling,
on the wind resounds Thy song.
Lead me onward,
ever upward,
to the land for which I long.

Sweet song of life,
sweet light of lights,
let me with Thy tide unite,
in Spirit blending,
Earth transcending,
far into Thy heavenly heights.

Oh mighty river
guide me ever
toward Thy shining central sea.
Within Thy laughter,
ever after,
let me find myself in Thee.

Chapter Three
Love

The Circle of Life
CONVERSATION AT THE INDIAN MOUNDS

I began to wonder how long the Chief planned to continue walking. I had expected to eat nearly two hours earlier. We'd already covered roughly a dozen miles and night had fallen. Instead, the Chief had led us on an uphill trek to where some "sacred stones" awaited. As I shuffled along through the darkness of a new moon, I could see the lantern the Chief had been swinging resting motionless on the ground ahead. He offered me a cup of water as I slumped wearily to the ground.

"These 'Indian Mounds' are a tourist attraction now," he said, almost in a whisper, "but you can still feel the power of this place. Most of these heavy stones were carried up the mountain from the banks of the Umpqua."

A sudden pang of fear rippled through my body as the Chief reached down and extinguished the lantern. My stomach rumbled a protest in the eerie silence. To our immediate right, I could still make out the mound of dark stones about six feet across.

"This is *a Place of Vision*," explained my guide. "My people also called it *a Place of Transformation*.

When a boy was making the transition into manhood, he would come up here early in the morning and fast all day. To further wear down the body, he would move these heavy stones from one pile to another. A thorough cleansing of body, mind, and spirit was necessary in order to induce a vision. This large pile of stones is all that's left. There used to be several smaller ones encircling it.

"During the vision quest, which would sometimes last several days and nights, the Great Spirit would appear as an animal, a bird, a strange being, or as a human. This powerful symbol either became a person's totem, serving as a protector, guide, or teacher throughout his life, or revealed a life-mission or spiritual purpose.

"I thought it might be interesting for us to go through a mini vision quest, since we were in the area. Thanks to our long day's hike we won't have to move any heavy stones," he added wryly.

"Oh, a vision quest," I responded, hoping to hide my reluctance behind a veil of enthusiasm... "that would be great." I wrapped myself securely in my blanket and closed my eyes. "No," my mind chattered, climbing a steep trail on an empty stomach at the end of an exhausting day's hike wasn't my idea of summer fun. A few feet away I could hear the Chief softly singing HU, the secret name of God. With any luck I would fall asleep before anything scary happened.

And then, amid powerful echoes from the past, under the dark and portentous new moon, seated where countless warriors had received their baptisms by fire, it happened. I fell asleep just as I'd planned.

I drifted in and out of a light sleep, tossing and turning on the hard, uneven ground. As was often the case when I didn't sleep well, my dream life was especially vivid. As I was falling asleep I noticed a bright yellow light dancing before my inner vision.

Yes, I was following a few steps behind the Chief in the dream. He was wearing a saffron robe. We were hiking through an evergreen forest interspersed with rainbow-colored dogwood trees. Each tree radiated light from jewel-clad branches and diamond-clustered leaves. It reminded me of a storybook land from a child's picture book. We stepped into a clearing where a man awaited us in the center of the lush green meadow.

The Chief put his hand on my shoulder as he spoke. "God always provides us with a teacher, one who can guide and protect us at every stage of our journey home to God. This is an old friend of yours. He first appeared in your life centuries ago, when you stood at a crossroads in your spiritual life. It was the beginning of an ages-long quest that has brought you here to this meadow," the Chief stated. "The continent where you first met has long since vanished beneath the waves of the Pacific."

The man wore a flowing blue robe and leather sandals. Stepping forward, he greeted us with keen brown eyes that were warm pools of dancing light. I felt great reverence and warmth for this man; however, the mists of time had erased his name and the circumstance surrounding our previous meeting from my memory.

"This land is called 'the Far Country,'" he stated, motioning with his hands. "A great many dimensions, or heavens, lie beyond the physical universe," he explained. "If we were sitting before an extended piano keyboard, the first seven notes would represent the physical plane. The next seven would represent the astral realm, and so on. The solid ground of the astral plane would be one key higher than the one representing the atmosphere of the Earth. This is why we can't see the inhabitants of the next world. Although you may recall this experience as a dream, we are presently in the mental plane, just beyond the astral.

"Beyond this mental realm lies the Soul plane, the first world where there is no duality or negativity. It is a realm of undivided light. Many of Earth's great teachers from the past make their home there, although God is many series of notes up the keyboard.

"Often those who desire to know God will meet their spirit guide in the dream state. The great mystery that every Soul must solve is this: God is every teacher that has ever crossed our path. Sometimes He takes the form of a totem, or animal guide, to help with a certain lesson; at other times God appears as Himself, the *Sat Guru,* to point the direction home. Meeting a true teacher of the highest order is a right that Soul earns through love and service. This marks Soul's greatest step toward self-awareness and divine love, the two things it has been seeking. Before this, Soul's success has been measured by its understanding of what love is not.

"Robert Frost, the American poet, wrote a two-line poem called *The Secret Sits:*

> We all dance round in a ring and suppose,
> but the Secret sits in the middle and knows!

"And what does this mean to us?" the teacher asked. He went on to explain.

"It means that we must enter into the heart of life, the very heart of God, in order to know what love really is. It is much more than the feeling between two people. When we associate love with a person, we run the risk of disappointment. That person may go out of our life through the door of death, or may leave us for another. Emotions of love can turn to bitterness in the face of rejection.

"Love is the greatest quality of God. It *is* God. Love is permanent, unconditional, and has no opposite. So, to know love we must know God. Since the reverse is also true, we can realize our dreams either through service or through understanding. These are the two great paths of love and wisdom."

The man smiled. "Your search for the Golden Heart has brought you here to this meadow. God can show you the narrow way into the Secret Kingdom in the center of the Circle of Life. All you need do is ask." He raised his right hand in a blessing. Then my dream scene changed.

The Chief and the man in the blue robe were gone. At the edge of the clearing a host of small children suddenly appeared. They were dressed in colorful costumes reminiscent of circus animals: elephants, lions, tigers, and bears. They joined hands, forming a large circle around me. A golden thread of love ran from heart to heart, uniting each one in the ring. A golden line of light also radiated from my own heart to each of the children, forming a hub.

They danced gleefully around the circle while singing the same verse over and over. With each chorus the golden light intensified and the melody became more enchanting. With each chorus the joy escalated, until a great feeling of love flooded the meadow. Finally, they broke formation and skipped single-file into the forest. But I could still hear the faint echo of their song as I roused myself from sleep:

> We are One in the Circle of Life.
> Love is All, just open your heart.
> We are One in the Circle of Life.
> Love is All, just open your heart...

I found the Chief kneeling before a pool in a nearby stream concealed behind an embankment a short distance away. He was splashing cool water on his face when I bounded down the hill and skidded to a stop. "Well, did you have any luck?" he called out.

After catching my breath, I recounted the events in as much detail as I could remember. I told the Chief about meeting the luminous being in the meadow, and his discourse on love. He conveyed his interest with a nod of approval. But when I told him about the adept's reference to my search for the Golden Heart, the Chief's eyes lit up with excitement. After I'd finished briefing him about the forest scene, he questioned me further about the Heart. Unfortunately, I had little to add.

While I'd found the reference to the Golden Heart interesting, it had been the costumed children dressed as circus animals that had captured my imagination. All in all, I was happy with the results of my first vision quest. The Chief seemed extremely pleased.

I told him that it had probably been beginner's luck. The dreams had been memorable, however, to say the least. As I reflected on the discussion of love, my mind drifted back to my grandmother's country church. At the urging of the minister, I had often attempted to love God. But, even by my own modest standards, I had failed miserably. I felt pretty guilty about it.

I asked the Chief if it was possible to love God. He said that it was, but added that most of us need more understanding of both love and God first. "Until we learn to love ourselves," the Chief explained, "our attempts at loving others, let alone God, will likely fall short. Love begins with understanding. When we understand the laws of creation and our own divine nature, then we discover ways of breaking through the barriers that separate us from love, like guilt, self-criticism, blame, and judgment.

"We're like sculptors," the Chief observed, "constantly chipping away at the outer facade of illusion that hides our true self. The reward for our perseverance is the perfection that lies at the center of our own being. This is the true home of God, our individual drop from the Ocean of Love. When we have gained this realization, we will then know both love and God."

The Masterpiece

A sculptor once came to live among the animals in a secluded valley of the Enchanted Forest. He had come to the forest for inspiration, to create a masterpiece to take back to the world of men. It would assure him his place among the masters of his craft, and it would bring him great wealth.

First, the artist spent days searching for just the right stone block from which to carve his monumental achievement. The cleaning and preparation of the rock took many weeks; but his patience paid off, for at last he stood before the awaiting capstone to his lifework.

But the artist was not yet ready to begin carving. Many months passed as he skillfully sharpened his chisels to the peak of perfection. Then, with hammer in hand, he circled the granite stone, gazing upon the finished piece in his imagination. A flicker of love ignited deep in his heart. At last a day came when he could no longer see a distinction between himself and the image surrounded by stone.

To the artist's surprise, his desire for riches had mysteriously vanished ... and no longer was he interested in the accolades of men. As he drew back his mallet, the artist remembered the many animals he'd come to cherish since his arrival. He dedicated this work to them.

One morning an osprey gave a startled cry. The news spread quickly—the artist was gone. But a beautiful sculpture stood in the middle of the meadow as his parting gift. Few had heard the ringing of a hammer or chisel, so quietly had the master craftsman gone about his business.

His greatest work of art was now complete, but the masterpiece had not been the image once bound in stone. It had been the image of perfection struggling to free itself from his own heart. As the artist made his way back to the city, he realized that he'd never found a suitable name for his greatest accomplishment.

Many seasons have passed over the rim of time since the day the unknown artist left the quiet valley. Squirrels now crack nuts on the base of the statue, while butterflies find rest on its outstretched arms. All the animals feel a great peace pouring from the wonderful gift left by their friend, the masterpiece they call *The Loving Heart.*

Sticks and Mud

One nesting season a sparrow built her home atop a flimsy branch that rose from the surface of a beaver dam. The other sparrows criticized the bird for choosing such a lowly and dangerous place to raise her young. What a poor reflection this would be on those who had built wisely in the regal fir and stately oak.

One cold winter day a terrible storm raged through the valley. Everything in its path was swept away, even the beaver dam—all but the tiny section where the sparrow had made her home. As the animals gathered to survey the damage, they cried out in disbelief. The tiny twig cradling the sparrow's nest had not been disturbed!

A multitude of curious sparrows gathered at the site of the miracle. The prophet noticed the bewildered birds and joined them.

"How," they asked him, "did the sparrow's nest survive? Even the great beaver dam of sticks and mud has been washed away by the flood."

"Things are not always as they appear," answered the prophet. "You see, the sparrow you looked down upon had a broken wing. For this reason, she was unable to build with the rest of you in the treetops. That is why she chose such a lowly place. While you could fly with the wind in search of fine materials for your home, the crippled sparrow could not. She lined the nest for her young with feathers from her own breast.

"It is one thing to build with sticks and mud," pointed out the prophet, "and yet another to build with love and sacrifice. Can you now understand why the sparrow's nest was spared?"

The Bridge Builder

A stranger once passed through the Enchanted Forest carrying a burlap knapsack and a string of fish. He stopped at the edge of a treacherous gorge. In the distance, the snow-capped peaks of the Purple Mountains glistened in the sun. He gazed wistfully at the horizon, beyond which, lay his homeland. Then, with a weary sigh, he forded the river where few others had crossed.

But once safe on that shore he did a strange thing. He began building a bridge. The animals watched in fascination as he went about his task. When at last he had finished, he set off again for his cherished destination.

Before he'd gone far, however, an eagle landed on the bridge and called after him. "Your crossing was difficult," he observed, "but you made it safely across. Why build a bridge now when it serves you no purpose?"

The man gave this answer: "I once met a child," he replied, "a fisherman like myself. One day he will cross here as I have done. This chasm is deep, and the river swift. It was difficult for me. At the time of his crossing his back will be crooked and his hair will be white. Out of love I've suspended this bridge for him. This bridge is for him and for the fishermen that follow."[7]

Swans Mate for Life

A porcupine approached his friend, the swan, asking advice about a gift for his beloved. For many years he'd watched the swans, wondering if they knew of a secret potion to make love last forever.

"There is a secret," confided the swan, "but you must never tell anyone where you heard of it. In the Valley of Illusion there grows a rare and beautiful flower called the 'heart-of-mine.' You'll recognize it by the heart that grows from its stem. Give this flower to your beloved and you will have her love always."

The porcupine thanked the swan, then set off on his quest for eternal love. After many hardships, he finally arrived at the hidden valley and found the delicate plant. With a trembling hand, he reached down to pluck the flower. But as he did, he heard a frail but beautiful voice.

"I hold the secret of eternal love," sang the flower. "It gives me great joy to pledge my heart to you forever...and in return I ask only this: When in my presence you must never admire another more beautiful than me; you must never listen to another more intelligent than me; and most importantly, you must never show your affection to another more loving than me."

The porcupine slowly drew back his hand. In a confused trot, he hurried back to Little River and walked in silence along its shore.

The mate of the swan spotted him from a distance and cried a tear. "For some the quest for love is too great a task," she exclaimed.

And tears also filled the eyes of the swan. "These tears are for love," he said in his heart, "whatever it might be."

One Moment of Indecision

How free it feels to fly
above the bustling crowds,
accompanied by solitude,
exploring worlds of flight
unfettered by desire.

There are skies so high
that all is golden light and ecstasy,
where lifetimes are but moments
on the face of time.

And there in a moment I see your eyes,
and hear a voice not so unlike your own
that whispers, "trade your wings for love,
though love may seem the strongest cage
in any universe."

Chapter Four
Tolerance

The Mountain of God
CONVERSATION NEAR EAGLE ROCK

I followed the Chief's gaze as I unwrapped a tuna fish sandwich. He was leaning across a redwood picnic table shielding his eyes. Ten miles to the north, the early afternoon sun reflected off the granite cliffs of Eagle Rock. Several black dots traced circles against its colorful facade. I knew they were buzzards, awaiting the passing of some weak animal in the timber below. I made a derogatory comment to the Chief about the appearance of buzzards, stating that I'd seen one up close.

"Do you mean to tell me you wouldn't invite one home for Sunday supper?" the Chief chided.

"I imagine God loves buzzards just as much as he loves swans or songbirds," he speculated, after a brief pause. "He knows their special purpose. Before we can tolerate their less-than-glamorous appearance we must first understand their purpose, as God does.

"When we see buzzards we think of our own mortality. God, on the other hand, views death only as the transition from motion to rest. Buzzards play a valuable role in His 'recycling business.' Remember God's two desires, the desire to set still ideas in motion, and the desire to return them once again to stillness?" I nodded in response.

The Chief continued. "It's reassuring to know that nothing happens to us by accident. Everything we experience is the result of thought. We are given the divine gift of imagination and the freedom to create our universe as we choose. There's just one stipulation—we must take responsibility for what we create.

"As gods of our own universe we are responsible for balancing every thought. Even though we'd like to believe it, there are no recording angels who occasionally fall asleep or go out for coffee when it is most convenient for us." I smiled at the image of a sleeping angel with a pencil tucked behind one ear. I could think of several instances when I wished that this had been the case, however.

"Each individual has his own 'electronic keynote,' his own cosmic signature. This identifying mark is stamped on every thought we send out. When we finally realize that our current circumstances are the result of past thoughts, then we stop blaming others for our problems. Self-responsibility is a milestone on our quest for love and freedom.

"When someone pushes our buttons, as they say, it is not the other person who is at fault. He is simply reflecting back what we have not recognized in ourselves. The *Mirror of Life* dutifully brings the contents of our Belief System to our attention. Until we are aware of this process, we will blame the messenger. We will miss a great opportunity to set things right. How can we release problems that we attribute to others?" The Chief paused briefly, allowing me to ponder his question.

"As an example of this reflection process, say we attract someone who continually takes advantage of our generosity. Most likely we have done the same to others in the past and are now learning what it feels like from the opposite point of view. To completely learn a lesson we must experience both sides of the coin."

I asked the Chief what was meant by "karma."

"This is what we've been talking about," he said. "When we send out thoughts that do harm to ourselves, others, animals, or nature, we must take responsibility for them at some later date. When that time comes, we balance those thoughts by experiencing the opposite viewpoint. We can also balance them by using our imagination. By couching the experience in mental pictures, we can gain the understanding while avoiding physical discomfort and inconvenience. When we understand the mechanics of creation, we can change our lives rather quickly. Change always begins with an inner process of awareness that is later reflected in our outer world.

"Wisdom comes from understanding our role as co-creators with God, and from experiencing all possible viewpoints. Many great things come from wisdom, but none more useful while living here on Earth than tolerance. It is another important key to Divine Love."

The Chief looked up at the massive stone bluff. "I climbed that mountain once," he recalled with noticeable satisfaction. "I must have been about twelve or thirteen at the time. One night in a dream I heard the screech of a golden eagle. It was perched on a dead snag on top of Eagle Rock, its wings outstretched. Eagle Rock symbolized the Mountain of God to my people. I believed the golden eagle was the Great Spirit calling for me.

"It took a full day and a great deal of effort to reach the top," the Chief explained. "I didn't find the eagle, but I did learn a valuable lesson."

The Chief peered over his peanut butter and jelly sandwich with twinkling eyes. "I learned that you can see much better from the top than you can from the forest below.

"You see," he continued, "those who have scaled the Mountain of God are tolerant of those still struggling on the path below, because they have seen life from both perspectives. Those fighting their way through the brambles of mediocrity often claim theirs is the only way to God. Due to cultural or religious biases, they condemn others who follow equally valid routes.

"Add to this drama the differences in people. Those who experience life primarily with their mind, for example, fail to appreciate those who *feel* their way through life. They say they are too emotional. Mental people are too cold and insensitive, the feeling people counter. What they don't realize is that both are legitimate means of perception: complementary, yet opposite, ends of the same stick."

I told the Chief that I understood the two different approaches to life all too well, and the resulting friction from their interaction. My father was a mining engineer, methodical, rigid, and businesslike. At the opposite extreme was my mother. She dabbled in painting and ceramics. Loving to dance, my mother was free flowing and intuitive, just the opposite of my outwardly directed and practical father. Neither fully understood nor appreciated the other's ways.

To further explain the wide variety of life-experiences, the Chief related a story about his first journey out-of-the-body. The Chief said he had roused from sleep one night around midnight to find his teacher, the Great Master, standing at the end of his bed. "He asked me if I would like to take a short journey to a Temple of Wisdom, a school, in the Himalayan Mountains," related the Chief.

"Still half asleep, the invitation didn't seem crazy at all, so I agreed. I took hold of his extended hand and suddenly found myself standing beside him looking back at my physical body in the bed. It was quite a shock, even though I had heard about such things. My teacher explained that I was now in my 'light body,' one similar in appearance to my physical body, yet finer in texture and vibrations. We lifted straight up in the air. He glanced over and smiled as I ducked my head to keep from hitting the ceiling. Imagine my surprise when we passed right through the roof!

"We rose higher and higher on invisible wings, until I lost sight of our tiny ashram. On the way to this school we crossed many mountains, as lakes and fields passed beneath us like polished mosaics. At last we came down on a narrow ridge that overlooked many valleys. The Temple of

Wisdom was located in the middle of a vast wilderness. But my teacher had been right. Traveling in the light body it had not been far at all.

"A wide walkway appeared to our right, one that led to a wooden structure clinging tenaciously to the side of the mountain. We walked down a long entry hall where the abbot of the monastery awaited us. He swung open a solid, double door and announced, 'Welcome to our School of Golden Wisdom. There are many others, as well, but they are a little further away.' He led me inside, then directed my attention to a great, circular mural painted on the domed ceiling."

I interrupted the Chief to ask him if leaving the physical body had been scary. He shook his head, "no," saying that it had been a joyous, free experience. He added that spiritual teachers protect their students so that no harm comes to them while studying at Schools of Golden Wisdom like this one. While in this instance he had been in the light body, the Chief pointed out that another, even higher, form of out-of-the-body travel existed. In this mode there was no detectable body, only a viewpoint from which to *see, know,* and *be.*

The Chief picked up his story where he'd left off. "The abbot, whose name was Rynnand Kymka, explained that the mural was called the *Wheel of Life.* Its illustrations depicted the different experiences Soul went through while on its sojourn here on Earth. In each of the twelve sections, or *nidanas,* Soul learned certain lessons, such as courage in the first round of experience, but also faced specific challenges.[8]

"Soul experienced self-gratification in another cycle, for example, while the lesson was self-discipline. By the twelfth cycle of experience, Soul sought liberation from the Wheel of Life. It yearned for home in the Ocean of Light.

"Since there are so many different types of people," pointed out the Chief, "you can see that a wide variety of experiences are available to Soul. Your father's experience in the first cycle, for example, would be different from your mother's.

"A possible courage-building experience would be war. As an engineer, your father would probably be involved with logistics. He might build a bridge to get troops and artillery into position. On the other hand, if your mother were placed in harm's way, she might find herself as a wartime correspondent. She might also capture the drama on canvas or on film."

The Chief concluded his story. "On this first visit to the Tibetan School of Wisdom, Rynnand Kymka urged me to follow my own course in life. He emphasized his point by stating, 'Giraffes don't roar like tigers, nor do they run like gazelles. God gave them special talents all their own.'

"'Soul plays many parts,' the abbot told me in parting. 'But Soul is not the characters it portrays so faithfully. Above all,' he said, *'Know Thyself.* We are eagles one and all, but we sleep like spiders in a web of dreams.'"

I looked up at the imposing presence of Eagle Rock, wondering if someday the eagle of Soul would call to me from its summit. At least that challenge would not be today, I consoled myself. Today I would enjoy the song of the river and the chocolate chip cookies my mom had packed for my excursion.

"Sometimes our journey treats us to beautiful meadows sprinkled with delicate flowers," observed the Chief. "At other times we must wend our way through dense forests, where few shafts of sunlight penetrate to the mossy floor. But every step of our journey is meticulously laid out prior to our incarnation. Complaining shows a lack of spiritual understanding, and limits our ability to love others and ourselves.

"While there is much to enjoy along the way," concluded my guide, "no one reaches the pinnacle of God without effort and sacrifice. And don't forget," he added with a laugh, "there are plenty of roots waiting to trip you up. A good sense of humor is a valuable asset. It can make your journey up the mountain much more tolerable."

A Path to Eagle Rock

A mountain goat stumbled upon a secret pathway that led to Eagle Rock. He was intoxicated by the breathtaking scenery, and marveled at his good fortune.

From out of the ethers came a voice. "This is the path of love. To walk this path is to sacrifice all, even unto death."

The mountain goat looked over the edge of the trail for the first time and spied the bones on the valley floor. As he hurried down the path, the mountain goat muttered to himself, "There must be other paths to Eagle Rock."

Porcupines at the Dance

In the *Year of the Bountiful Grains,* under the full moon of the celestial equinox, the creatures of the forest gathered for their harvest dance. Before long, everyone was caught up in the festive mood. The sound of laughter and merriment could be heard from afar.

The porcupines, with their keen minds and technical knowledge of dance, were soon coaching others on the more difficult steps.

"You might swing your hips a bit more, Mr. Badger," one called. "The foxtrot is a dance of controlled exuberance."

Confident in their own ability, the porcupines often pushed themselves to the limit while attempting difficult moves. Occasionally, however, one would stumble wildly, much to the horror of the other dancers.

At dawn the gathering broke up, and the porcupines sauntered up the trail to their homes in a state of ecstasy, for their greatest pleasure came from dancing.

As they disappeared into the forest a deer commented, "The porcupines are such wonderful dancers. They certainly add color to our annual gatherings."

The badger spoke out with hurt feelings. "Yes, but you'd think with their analytical minds they could see that badgers aren't blessed with their agility for dancing, and would be less critical."

A bear held one arm. "There is a fine line between analytical thinking and being critical," he observed. "It's a shame those porcupines are so insensitive at our gatherings and stumble about so!"

Buzzards at the Potluck

A group of buzzards showed up at the memorial service of a deer that had recently been hit by a logging truck. Much to the surprise of all, the buzzards proved to be sensitive and compassionate, mourning the passing of the deer in as sincere a manner as anyone in attendance.

"Although we live apart from the other animals of the forest," one buzzard explained to a bear, "we look upon every creature as a brother. Our differences are largely a matter of culture, not of belief."

The bear was moved by what was said, and asked the buzzard to be a guest speaker at the next worship service. He also invited the vulture's family to attend a potluck following the meeting.

At the worship service, some were put off at the appearance of the buzzard. It was the first time many of the worshipers had observed a buzzard from such close proximity. But as he spoke with such wisdom and eloquence, the members of the congregation glanced at each other approvingly.

"We believe in one God, as you do," sang out the buzzard, "although we call Him by a different name.

"We follow religiously the principle of 'sow what you would reap.' We believe as you do, that Soul is reborn into greater and ever greater body forms... and that thoughts of truth build upon themselves. Perhaps one day it will be discovered that thought is creative, and that we can design our own heaven while still on Earth by the thoughts we think."

The assembly was amazed and properly moved by the great insights of the buzzard, and accepted him without qualification as a brother in their hearts.

At the potluck, a variety of nuts, berries, and delicacies from both stream and woodland graced the long table where the animals sat. The crowd was buzzing over the insight they had just been given on the power of thought. At last the bear stood up with paw raised, signaling for silence preceding the blessing of the food.

But just as the bear lifted his head in reverence, the silence was broken by a loud smacking sound from the end of the table. One by one every head turned. The animals reeled in horror at what they saw. In a state of frenzy, the buzzards were ripping and tearing at the hindquarters of the deer they had brought to the potluck.

After the buzzards had gone and the gathering had dispersed, many of the more devoted creatures stayed well into the night. Praising the new insight on creative thought, they vowed to see it through to its application.

"Let us build our heaven on a foundation of equality," called the bear.

"And let us build our heaven in a region of perpetual spring," added the squirrels. A murmuring of approval swept through the crowd.

"And let us build our heaven in the spirit of brotherhood," spoke the falcon. Many heads nodded in agreement, as silence testified to their sincerity.

From far in the back a barely audible voice added, "And let us build our heaven as far away from the heaven of the buzzards as God will allow."

In unison, a cry burst forth, "AMEN!"

The Big Game

The rabbits of Little River met the Bristol Prairie squirrels for a game of baseball. Before the game started, however, a loud quarrel broke out.

"The bases are too far apart," protested the squirrels.

"Your rulebook is incorrect," shouted a rabbit. "It was changed long ago by a short-legged squirrel who had no respect for the sacred game of baseball. Squirrels today have longer legs and can play by the proper rules, the rules of the rabbits."

After a long discussion, the rabbits conceded and the game was begun. But when the rabbits came up to bat the argument erupted again. "You're running the wrong way," cried the squirrels. "You're supposed to run from home to first, not from home to third."

"We've always run this way," shouted a rabbit. "It's written in our rulebook."

In spite of the confusion, the game progressed. The rabbits ran the wrong way and the squirrels insisted on using two sets of bases. By the third inning, however, neither side could agree on the correct score and a big fight was brewing.

Just as things were about to explode, a falcon flew down and lit on home plate. "The badgers are playing a new game called 'football' up at Horse Heaven," he reported. "It's even more ridiculous than your game."

"Whaaat!" exclaimed a squirrel. "There's only supposed to be one game played in this forest."

"It's in our rulebook too," agreed the captain of the rabbits, puffing out his chest. "We'll soon put an end to *that* game."

Circus

There are many jobs to choose from
   in this circus we call life.
Some require a brighter spotlight;
   some command a higher price.

But what matters is the giving—
   not the money, not the fame.
It's what we've learned, not how we've learned it,
   when the tents are put away.

But sometimes I wish I had
   a more important job to do.
Sometimes I dream I'm out there
   in the spotlight next to you.

I pretend that I'm the bravest flyer
   on the high trapeze.
I'm the man who trains the tigers;
   lions cower at my feet.

I'm balanced on the tight rope
   and they're cheering down below.
I'm the clown, then I'm the juggler.
   I'm the man who runs the show.

Then it's back to what I'm doing.
   I hear someone call my name.
I hear someone say I'm needed
   in the Big Top right away.

I clean up behind the elephants.
   I put them in their stall.
As for you, I guess you'll always
   be the human cannonball.

But does it matter what I shovel,
   does it matter where you fall,
if it's love that we discover
   at the bottom of it all?

Chapter Five
Discrimination

A Prospector's Cabin
CONVERSATION AT THE MINER'S SHACK

"Be clear on what you desire," advised the Chief. "If you aren't clear, you run the risk of being controlled by someone with a stronger will."

We were hiking along one of the many small streams that fed the North Umpqua from the Bohemia Basin, famous for its gold rush in the early 1900's. The Chief had planned this detour to visit an old prospector's cabin about three miles off the main road. From the Chief's description, I half expected to find the porch light on and the smell of fresh-baked bread greeting us down the trail. Instead, to our disappointment, we found the dwelling on the verge of collapse.

"I knew most of the prospectors along these tributaries," recalled the Chief, scraping some moss from an encrusted picnic table. "They were my teachers in a way." The old traveler surveyed the ravaged banks of the stream. He then gazed out at the horizon in silence, remembering the glory days of the Bohemia Basin, or perhaps acknowledging the fleeting faces of old friends parading before his inner vision. At last, he tossed a handful of moss on the ground and continued.

"I discovered that all these prospectors had at least two things in common. They were all fierce individuals, and they were all clear on what they wanted. Of course they were driven by their desire for gold; but I also found the same qualities present in the lives of the saints.

"When I discovered for myself how simply a miner could live," he went on, "I began to examine my true needs. I got clear on what I had to have to survive, and what desires would make me happy. In a word, I learned to discriminate. Individuals discriminate. This is what gives them a certain amount of power in this world. What they accomplish is determined by two things — where they place their attention, and how much feeling they put into their dreams.

"To be free we must be able to discriminate; but to discriminate we must be free. This paradox simply means that we must first clean out the limiting beliefs that daily shape our lives before we can begin to see clearly enough to discriminate properly.

"You might be surprised to know that many religious leaders and government officials understand the power of thought, and use it to control the masses. We're led to believe that we need to be taken care of, body, mind, and Soul. From an early age, education molds us into conforming members of society. *Conforming* is the key word here.

"Self-appointed religious authorities mislead us into believing that we are wretched sinners. Their scriptures mix in just enough truth to make the misinformation palatable. While politicians promise security, then proceed to take away our freedom, from the pulpit priests use fear to modify behavior. It's in their best interest to keep us in the dark. Our divine birthright and the great power we wield to create our own reality are closely guarded secrets.

"When we forgot how to build our castles in the air, we began throwing up cardboard lives that needed to be insured, protected, and repaired. Today most churches and governments will gladly provide everything needed to build a cardboard life. From an early age we are trained to need and desire society's offerings. Believe me, society would rather shape us into consumers than individuals. Consumers are more easily controlled.

"New ideas are dangerous to those in power unless they can be subverted to further their control over the masses. Control goes deeper than you can begin to imagine. Generally new ideas aren't a great problem for those in power, however, for human nature clings to tradition. The old rut feels comfortable and safe; to change takes effort."

The Chief walked down to the bubbling stream and seated himself on a patchwork quilt of white-petaled daisies and yellow buttercups. "Things haven't always been like they are today, Michael," he observed, shaking his head. "Once we were competent builders. But a secret battle has been going on, a battle for the imagination. We have all been given the sacred gift of imagination to build how we choose. But we've become lazy builders. We let 'outside authorities' do our thinking for us."

I remembered the ending to a popular hymn from my grandmother's church: "...*for such a worm as I."* Probably not the best foundation for building self-esteem! I wondered what other second-hand information I had blindly accepted about myself. If the Chief was right, my whole Belief System had been built on false assumptions about success, health, happiness, knowledge, salvation, and no doubt much more. I began to see the value of questioning tradition, especially where money and power were concerned.

"Is there a way to know for sure what is true?" I asked.

"Fortunately there is," answered the Chief. "We can establish our own *self-knowledge* through contemplation. This involves using our imagination to form a picture in the mind's eye. To begin with, we might imagine ourselves on a brightly lit stage examining whatever it is we want to know more about. The images don't have to be exact, but they should include things we're already familiar with.

"All we are doing is holding our attention on the problem or concept so our Higher Self can take a look at it. Our true self views it from all angles, then files the information away as self-knowledge in our higher mind. This area is sometimes called the subconscious. Next, we must trust that our answer is actually there within us. At this point, we won't have conscious knowledge.

"Since we have temporarily lost contact with our subconscious, we need to find a way to retrieve the data. Some will rely on flashes of intuition. Others will get their answer in a dream. In some cases we will wake up in the morning and 'just know' what course to take. Many times our outer life will tell us the answer. We may be led to a book, or perhaps a friend will call and 'coincidentally' mention just the right thing.

"Synchronicity often involves this type of communication from our Higher Self. Some call these meaningful coincidences *waking dreams*.[9] After contemplating on a problem or an idea, watch where your attention is drawn as you go about your day.

"To give you an example, once I was seeking an answer to a health problem. Less than an hour after putting the issue into picture form, a water line broke leading into my house. Later that morning a flyer came in the mail announcing that it was 'Water Week.' A third water symbol came up that night.

"I turned to a talk radio program and absentmindedly listened as I went about my evening chores. The guest was talking about the dangers of dehydration. Since the water theme had come up earlier, the discussion caught my attention. I realized that my Higher Self was telling me to drink more water."

I followed the Chief back up the trail to the miner's shack, reflecting on outside authorities. Other than my hiking companion, I had never heard anyone talk about "mental bondage" before. I suddenly realized what could happen if I continued to allow others to do my thinking for me.

Dusky light streamed in through the broken window behind the Chief. With a furrowed brow, he solemnly studied the contents of the cabin. Normally silence is accompanied by a feeling of emptiness. This silence, however, felt heavy. I envisioned a room bursting with a thousand memories, all awakening at once. The Chief picked up a small key lying nestled among some old *Life* magazines, then, ever so carefully, placed it on a tiny nail behind the battered door.

I noticed a faded, yellow hair ribbon pressed snugly up against an old alarm clock with a cracked face. Time had stopped at eleven fifty-eight. The Chief followed my gaze. "The minutes are more important than the years," remarked the old traveler with a hint of melancholy, "...the moments are most important of all. Things change," he said quietly, glancing down at his worn shoes, "whether we want them to or not. All we have is the present moment."

Through a section of missing roof, I glanced up at the darkening clouds. Rain was on its way. I could tell the cabin had stirred more memories than the Chief had chosen to reveal. The next big windstorm would no doubt level the structure, and this part of the Chief's life would move further into the mist as did ancient Avalon.

John Redstone closed the door, then turned to survey the site one last time. With a telling backward glance he started down the trail. "We'd better head for home," he called back.

The Tricks of a Fox

A fox found a book alongside a trail called *The Secrets of the Universe.* Wherever he went thereafter, the fox would carry the book on his back or balance it upon his nose. Although he couldn't read, he would sometimes sit at the foot of the Giant Oak in the center of the forest and pretend to do so.

In time the fox became somewhat of a celebrity, for in addition to his balancing act, he also mastered the art of catching the book in his mouth after tossing it high in the air. Many were blinded by his charismatic demonstrations, and fell into believing that the greatest secrets of the universe consisted only of clever tricks.

While it's true that few were actually fooled by the deceptions of the false teacher, he did manage to lure a small, loyal following of rabbits to his monastery in a remote valley. The owls, realizing that nothing is more dangerous than knowledge subverted to selfish purposes, tried to warn the devotees of the devious fox. But his charm held them spellbound.

Two of the rabbits did finally return to Bristol Prairie, but the rest of the group mysteriously disappeared without a trace.

The Subversive Side of Gophers

Dorinda lived in a small cottage at the edge of the forest. She loved all the animals, but especially the gophers because they had such refreshing ideas.

One morning Dorinda watched her mother preparing breakfast. Very carefully she cut both ends off the bacon before putting it in the large frying pan. "Why do you always cut the ends off the bacon, Mother?" Dorinda asked. "There's still so much room in the pan."

"This is the way we've always cooked bacon, Dear. It's the proper way."

Dorinda shook her head. "It seems like such a waste!" she exclaimed.

"Why, you've been listening to those gophers again, haven't you?" her mother cried. "I thought I told you to stay away from their kind. They have such strange ideas."

The following Sunday Dorinda visited her grandmother's house and helped with the breakfast. Very carefully Dorinda cut both ends off the bacon as her mother had done. "Why do we always cut the ends off the bacon, Grandmother?" she asked.

"Why, it's the way we've always cooked bacon, Dear. It's the proper way." She reached down and took out a tiny pan. "And besides, it's the only way it will fit in the pan."

"Grandmother," Dorinda observed, "if you would buy a bigger pan you wouldn't have to cut the ends off the bacon. You would save money."

Dorinda's grandmother turned on her. "It sounds like you've been listening to those gophers again. It's no wonder things are in such a mess today. You mark my word, those gophers would undermine the whole world if they thought they could get away with it."[10]

The Secret Language

An owl and a possum followed a bubbling stream past a beaver dam to where it emptied into a sunlit river. "The Great Spirit has revealed to me a secret language with which we can communicate with one another," confided the owl. "He has told me that most creatures only sleep, dreaming they are awake. It is time to wake up, to open our eyes and see that life here is only a dream." The possum looked at the owl through narrow slits of eyes, wondering what he was talking about.

"For example," the owl said, "Did you see the newborn fawn we just passed? The Great Spirit was telling me that a new cycle of prosperity is beginning for me. We must learn to interpret these waking dream symbols as we would the symbols in our dreams, and come to an agreement with the Great Spirit on their meaning.

"And can you see the sunlight reflecting upon the water downstream like a million diamonds? Those diamonds shall be my treasure in old age, a reward for living a life free of anger.

"And there," the owl pointed, "upon the shore where the river bends, can you see that perfect tree growing from the surface of the old stump?

That is my favorite tree. It reveals my immortality, for I shall be reborn into a new form more perfect than the one I now wear."

The possum looked upon the owl with admiration, for such thoughts as symbols had never occurred to him. On the way home his step was a happy step, for, if he understood correctly, his great dream was now within reach.

That night, silhouetted against a full moon, a strange creature could be seen standing high upon a cliff overlooking Bristol Prairie. A voice sang out reverently, thrice repeating an affirmation. "Hear me, oh Great Spirit. Let these fir boughs tied to my arms be my wings of glory!" Thus saying, he sprang from the cliff.

The next morning, while everyone talked about the unusual spectacle from the night before, the possum was hanging from an oak branch with his back to the others, moaning under his breath.

As angry footsteps approached, the possum became very still, pretending to be asleep. The owl stomped past the group muttering to himself about the uncertainty of the future and the mischievousness of beavers.

"What has disturbed the owl so this beautiful morning?" asked a bobcat.

"It seems," whispered the bear, so as not to awaken the possum, "that someone has chopped down his favorite tree."

At the Crossroads of Life

An old prospector met a muskrat at the crossroads of life. "How are you?" asked the muskrat.

"Not well," complained the miner. "I've come from the mountains where the strange flower grows. My search was in vain for the gold I have dreamed of."

"Tell me more of the flowers," inquired the muskrat.

"They are strange flowers, indeed," replied the prospector. "From the stem grows three hearts. One heart grows with wisdom, another with power, and the third grows with freedom. The flower that blooms is the perfection of love. 'Tis a flower of the gods, but worth nothing to me. And how goes your life?"

"Not well," answered the muskrat, "for truth has escaped me. I'm moving to the mountains. I've left everything behind in my house of gold." The muskrat pointed toward the bend in the river. "I'm certain things will improve for you," he called back.

"And for you," returned the prospector, as he took his leave. After the muskrat was out of sight, the miner ran for his treasure.

"What fools are those muskrats," he muttered to himself. From deep in the mountains came a squeal of delight.

The coins of heaven and Earth are seldom interchangeable.

Buttercup

The moments hurry by
too swift to hold,
until I catch them in a cup of gold.

And soon the edges swell
with glistening spheres,
looking more like dewdrops than like years.

Then beauty overflows
upon a world,
dawning on a petal softly curled.[11]

Chapter Six
Giving

The Dream Catcher
CONVERSATION AT THE STILL POND

Besides settling the dust, the summer rain revitalized the parched forest and enlivened its thirsty inhabitants. A fine mist fell as we set up our crude camp beside a small pond created by a beaver dam. After we had left the cabin, the Chief led us cross-country along a once-familiar deer trail now overgrown with scotch broom. We came out at dusk on a small stream that emptied into Steamboat Creek, a tributary of the North Umpqua.

It took us about twenty minutes to construct a temporary shelter out of fir boughs and a lightweight tarp we carried with us. As he had done before, the Chief carefully removed from his pack a black leather ring decorated with seven colored feathers. Shiny, black, obsidian beads separated the feathers. He then fastened it above the open entrance.

The Chief explained that it had been a gift from his grandfather. He called it a "dream catcher." Traditionally it was placed above the door to protect the occupant from harm and to attract spiritual dreams. The circle, he said, represented the dreamer's consciousness, the gateway into the world of dreams. It was also an invitation to your spirit guide.

"The spirit of a gift is as important as the gift itself," pointed out the Chief. "This dream catcher was given with the divine vibration of love. This is why I've had it for so long. I've received many gifts in my life, but have kept only a few. Some gifts were given from a sense of duty. Others were given with an expectation of something in return. Because of this, they didn't stand the test of time. The gifts given without love either wore out, broke, or were lost.

"I also discovered that it is important how a gift is accepted, as well. A gift given with love and sacrifice, no matter what it might be, should be received in a spirit of gratitude, even if it is kept only briefly."

I gazed out upon the still water behind the dam. It was twilight. With the gentle rain, a spirit of contentment had settled over the marshy plain. The robust song of a bullfrog resounded from the thick cattails below us.

I asked the Chief why people give so little.

"The main reason we don't give freely," he explained, "is due to *fear*. We're afraid we won't have enough left for ourselves if we give some away. It's a pattern deeply ingrained in our Belief System from many lifetimes of struggle and mis-understanding. We've forgotten that the universe is abundant beyond measure. It operates on the Law of Giving, or Rhythmic Balanced Interchange. One polarity gives to its opposite, which, in turn, re-gives its energy to its counterpart. Receiving also is important.

"Our trouble receiving," continued my companion, "can be traced to *self-worth*. If we have judgments of unworthiness in our Belief System, all the abundance of the universe can come to us, but it will do us no good. It will fall right through our fingers. This applies to wealth, but even more importantly, to love and happiness.

"To recap for a moment. Removing these judgments is a simple matter. A higher understanding will automatically transmute a judgment of lower frequency. We must use mental pictures, or imagination, to establish self-knowledge. Imagine a pyramid. We simply add bits of truth to the top, then wait for the old judgments to settle out the bottom. In reality, we are re-writing the rules we have agreed to live by. It is also important to release any trapped emotional pain we may be holding."

The haunting cry of a loon drifted through the twilight, harmonizing well enough with the growing chorus of frogs. About three hundred fifty yards to our north a doe and her fawn were drinking. In the final afterglow of the day, I could just make out the faint ripple on the surface of the dark pond made by the nose of an approaching muskrat. I wondered what other animals were silently studying their uninvited guests?

All my life I had been haunted by fears of abandonment and, like many of my peers, struggled with feelings of inadequacy and low self-esteem. As I fell asleep to the sound of rain pelting nearby maple leaves, I asked my spirit guide to show me something from my past relating to these painful issues. It was difficult asking for help. I was even a bit skeptical that anything would happen.

To my surprise, however, my spirit guide *did* appear once again. He looked exactly as he had appeared in the meadow, the same blue robe and leather sandals. Flashing a reassuring smile, he proceeded to lead me down a long hallway in silence. Finally, we stopped in front of a door marked "Swiss Life." And thus began my painful introductory course on the eternal nature of Soul. I was about to learn how the threads of my past had woven the blanket I now slept beneath.

"This was an important time for you, Michael," the Dream Guide explained. "The seeds of your abandonment issue were sown here." As if watching a scene from a three-dimensional movie, I saw myself as a middle-aged man, the father of three children. My wife and I were seated at an empty dinner table, arguing loudly. As usual, my pursuit of pleasure at the local pub had left the family in dire straits. We didn't know where our next meal was coming from.

A sense of sadness and regret flooded my consciousness. I saw myself shirk my responsibility to my family in favor of self-indulgence in scene after scene. After abandoning my wife and children, that lifetime ended in sorrow, loneliness, and addiction.

"Self-responsibility was your main lesson here," pointed out my guide, without condemnation. "As Soul, we are given many chances to get it right. Let's look a bit further ahead."

Passing through another door, I saw myself as a Tibetan boy of eight, clad in a tattered brown robe. I was standing alone at a monastery gate. With tears blurring my vision, I watched my parents disappear down the long road we had just traversed. As I waited in the darkness for the abbot of the monastery to receive me, a crushing feeling of abandonment weighed heavily on my heart. I felt unloved, thrown away, and worthless.

"It was the last time you would see your father and mother in that life," explained my guide. "Although not a happy one, your austere life as a monk was a successful one. You paid back much of your debt to the universe for abandoning your family in the Swiss Alps. Some emotional scars still remain, however. Additionally, you made progress with self-discipline, and took on small tasks to help build self-responsibility. We'll keep working on that one," he said, offering a compassionate smile.

Truth isn't always pretty or neatly packaged like a box of chocolates. Somehow, I had convinced myself that my low self-esteem and fear of abandonment could be traced to a source other than my own past actions. This was a shocking wake-up call for me. My Dream Guide must have sensed that I'd seen enough for the time being. I spent the remainder of the night walking alone through a peaceful garden somewhere in an unknown region of the Far Country.

The next morning I awoke at dawn and quietly slipped from the shelter. As I reflected on my choices of the past, I absentmindedly tossed a few pebbles in the quiet pond. One by one the ripples slowly churned their way toward shore with mechanical precision. Deep down, I knew that the Law of Cause and Effect was equally as precise.

A Raccoon's Gift

A raccoon gave a gift to his beloved. She thanked her admirer, but then left the tiny shell on a rock as she took her leave.

After she had gone, the prophet spied the disheartened raccoon sitting alone on the riverbank. He noticed the unique shell and asked to examine it. As he turned it over and over in his hand, he realized that it had come from the ocean more than sixty miles downstream.

The prophet was very touched, for he now understood the measure of the raccoon's offering. The true gift had not been the shell at all. It had been the long walk.

Given to Love

One day a priest stopped by the cabin of the prophet asking for donations. The money, he explained, would buy chairs for his church. The name of each donor was to be inscribed on a brass plate, then attached to the back of each chair in recognition of the giver.

The prophet knew that a sincere man stood before him. He also knew that many in the minister's congregation would benefit from listening to his simple words each Sunday. He responded that he would be happy to donate a chair to his church in the valley.

The grateful priest thanked the prophet for his generous gift. "And what name shall we inscribe on the back of your chair?" he asked.

The prophet wrote down three words on a piece of paper, then folded it. "Please inscribe this on the back of the chair in your temple of God," he requested.

The priest thanked him again, then returned to his church without reading the paper he carried with him in his vest pocket. The following day he gave the still-folded paper to a man skilled in the art of inscription, along with the names of the other donors.

At last the day came when the chairs arrived. Through the tiny stained-glass window the devoted priest could be seen passing down each row. He stopped first behind one chair and then another, repeating a blessing for each of the benefactors.

Finally the priest stepped up to the last chair in the back row. He carefully studied the polished brass plate, then, with a smile of approval, knelt down and said a special prayer for the anonymous donor. The inscription simply read *"Given to Love."*

The Eagle and the Falcon

One afternoon an eagle and a falcon were engaged in a philosophical discussion near the top of the Giant Oak.

Said the eagle, "I agree with you, Mr. Falcon, if the creatures of the forest were more honest with one another, kinship would be the order of the day." Before the falcon could reply, the disharmonious screech of a jaybird echoed through the forest. Even as the cry went forth, a hungry mountain lion had been poised to devour the distracted birds. But seconds after the warning the two birds were airborne, well beyond the reach of its powerful paws.

Safe in the bough of a tall pine, the eagle, overcome by feelings of gratitude, called out to the jay, "Would you care to join us, Mr. Jay? We were just discussing the importance of giving from the heart, and not from a sense of duty."

And so the three sat, long after the moon had ushered in the night. Beneath the tree, many of the lesser creatures of the forest could be seen huddled in the shadows, hoping to gather a few crumbs of wisdom.

But as the evening progressed, much to the dismay of all, the jay dominated the conversation with his senseless chattering. Occasionally, when the jay would pause long enough to draw another breath, the eagle would politely nod his great head and say, "That's very interesting, Mr. Jay." And the falcon would interject, "I'm so glad you could join us." But both in their hearts were saying, "Indeed, it would be better to be eaten by mountain lions than to long endure the chattering of these jaybirds!"

At Journey's End

A footbridge near the source of the North Umpqua sent for an eagle. "Please carry this question to the bridge near the river's mouth for me," he requested. "We have grown old together, yet our destinies have kept us apart. Please ask my friend what great lesson he has learned from life."

The eagle flew with the wind, and soon lit on the great bridge near the mouth of the Umpqua. "Your friend, the footbridge near the river's source, sends his regards. He has instructed me to ask you what great lesson you have learned from life."

The bridge spoke to the eagle in a tone of importance. "Tell my friend this," he commanded. "Long ago, in my youth, a wealthy merchant returned to his homeland from a distant country. He taught me a valuable lesson. In his possession were precious oils and fragrances, enough to fill a hundred clay vessels. Many merchants have followed in this man's footsteps. Tell my friend I've learned this: 'To gain wealth one must not be afraid of leaving home. Wealth may be measured by what has been sacrificed to gain it.'

"Now tell me," he inquired, "how is my friend, the footbridge?"

"He is well," answered the eagle, "and sends this message that I recount for you now in his own humble words.

"Once, in my youth, a man passed by at the end of his journey. He had nothing left but a gold-colored vessel, for as he had traveled, he'd given all he owned to the poor along the way. When he laid his empty vessel at my feet he told me this: 'Our true home is far away, and often we must sacrifice all we own to reach it.'

"Few have followed in this man's footsteps," observed the footbridge, "although many years have passed since that fateful day. From him I learned this: The true measure of a man is in the amount he holds to give, not in the amount he holds to gain."

Content Is the Footbridge

Content is the footbridge over the stream,
    the one I sometimes sit beside,
while others pass in search of dreams,
    pursuing rivers flowing clear
to ocean shores that draw them near.

But I've found rivers far too wide,
    and crossing oceans can be rough.
Some have crossed them, undenied,
    but I've found streams to be enough.

Chapter Seven
Humility

The Proving Grounds
CONVERSATION AT BRISTOL PRAIRIE

"Many kids grow up believing that love is the reward of perfection," remarked the Chief. "Every parent wants to see his child do well, but some put far too much pressure on their kids to succeed. Few are able to get straight A's, or win the game with a last second touchdown pass.

"Success is like a shovel, Michael. It can uncover a treasure, or it can dig us a hole! We can measure our success in life by the strength of our desire to share our treasure with others. Our accomplishments can be tarnished when the ego gets involved. We can find ourselves in a spiritual hole."

The Chief chuckled, perhaps recalling an event from his own life. "It sometimes takes a good lesson in humility to get us back on solid ground. We all need to fumble the ball on the one yard line occasionally. It makes us appreciate the good times, and feel a little compassion for the losers."

I knew the Chief was right. In Junior High School I'd made a basket for the opposing team. I still remembered it like it was yesterday. My teammates have never forgotten it either.

"Love is its own reward," continued the Chief. "Only a true master can find perfection in this dark world. It's not because he is without flaws, or because he attends a service once a week. It's because he sees the wholeness, and therefore the holiness, of life. He sees the interplay between the positive and negative polarities as the dance of the Great Spirit. He has realized that all life is spiritual, all life is in divine order."

We rested on the edge of a high plain called Bristol Prairie. Its rugged beauty was unrivaled; yet a lonely solitude permeated the place. The Chief had described Horse Heaven as its name implied, with herds of wild horses thundering across open fields of golden grasses. By contrast, here one might expect to see a large bull elk step out of an embankment of fog.

Somewhere below us, beyond earshot, the eternal North Umpqua was churning its way through steep canyons of Douglas Fir toward the Pacific. The Chief and I were winded from the long climb. We leaned back against a giant pine, enjoying the comfort of a spongy moss blanketing the ground.

Moss also covered the trunk of the tree, but only the north side, the one nourished by the moist south wind. The Chief told me that tree moss could be used to tell directions in the absence of a compass.

"My people struggled with the pressure to succeed, also," he continued. "We called this place, Bristol Prairie, 'The Proving Grounds.' It was *a Place of Testing,* where young warriors put their survival skills to the test. Great mock battles were staged here. At other times the warriors in training had to overcome the elements by building temporary shelters from whatever they could find. Sometimes they were brought here without food or water in the dead of night, and were left to fend for themselves. The ones who fared the best had a strong sense of self-worth and self-confidence. They became the leaders.

"Balance is the test of leadership. An exaggerated sense of self-importance can easily turn to vanity. A saint must walk the razor-edged path with both confidence and humility, just like a good leader.

"My grandfather was a good role model for me when I was very young. We spent a lot of time together. He told me that I would be successful in life if I did two things: If I followed through on what I said I would do, and, if I did it on time, when I said I would do it. This was his simple formula for becoming a holy person."

I asked the Chief if he considered himself a saint. He laughed with surprise at this, shaking his head. "I'm just a tired old man nearing the end of his journey," he exclaimed. He reached in his pocket and took out a shiny black stone.

"I'm like this ancient piece of obsidian," he said, handing it to me. "It's been transmuted by volcanic fire, broken down by countless storms, and then chipped into the rough shape of this arrowhead. It finally became useful in a small way." The Chief surveyed the semi-barren plain.

"I've come to the conclusion that people crave two things: to feel loved, and to feel useful. You'd probably find a few of these arrowheads here on

Bristol Prairie," he stated, changing the subject.

"I used to think about this place a lot when I was living overseas," he continued. "It's funny how we seldom appreciate things until we're separated from them. We usually take for granted the people closest to us in our lives."

I asked the Chief if he missed India.

"Oh, not the country, itself," he said. "But when I returned to the States I did miss the evening *satsangs* with the Great Master. Satsangs are meetings where spiritual subjects are discussed or studied. My teacher was one in a million. You could feel an aura of love several hundred yards from his retreat near *Beas* (pronounced BAY-us) as you approached. I learned a lot about love and humility from him.

"People came from every corner of the world, and brought all their problems with them. The Master always sat on a thin mat in the middle of the floor so he could meet them at eye level. He didn't want to appear above them in any way. Buddhists, Christians, Muslims, whatever the person's religious background, it didn't matter. He would take the time to answer every question with great care and respect.

"Everyone felt loved by the Master, not only his disciples. It was once said of him that every person who left his presence — man, woman, or child — walked away thinking to himself, 'he loves me the most!'[12] He became a famous guru in that part of the world, even though fame was something the Great Master shunned."

I thought to myself how the things the Chief had said about his Indian teacher could also be said about him. It was ironic that truly great teachers towered above the rest because they refused to put themselves above even the most simple person.

"All World Teachers are unique individuals," explained the Chief, after a brief pause. "Some have an aptitude for teaching; others are more comfortable working behind the scenes. The Great Master had a quiet strength. On the other hand, I've met other masters who radiated great personal power. Their unique characteristics are tailored to fit the missions they have chosen.

"Alice Bailey told the world about the Seven Rays of Life.[13] These are the seven colors we see when white light is passed through a prism. Red, blue, and yellow, the three primary colors, correspond with the first three emanations from the Divine: the Ray of Power, the Ray of Love/Wisdom, and the Ray of Abstract Intelligence.

"The Fourth Ray, the green ray, is the Ray of Art. Musicians, painters, writers, and dancers, all draw their inspiration from this source. The Fifth Ray, the Building Ray, is orange; the Sixth Ray, the Ray of Devotion, is indigo in color. The Seventh Ray is known as the Ray of Unity, and radiates a violet hue. Seventh-Ray people are very orderly in nature.

"We are happiest when we find a career that is in harmony with the predominant ray in our makeup. Every aspect of our being vibrates in accordance with one or more of the seven rays. Being an artist and a writer, for example, you would feel stifled working as an accountant or as a mathematician, both Third-Ray occupations. Neither would you enjoy police work, or the political arena. These are associated with the First Ray of Life.

"Each ray has its strengths, but also its weaknesses. Many artists struggle with similar problems: self-confidence, self-responsibility, addiction, and balance. These tests are common to Fourth-Ray individuals.

"Our *Atma,* or Soul, can only come into existence on one of the first three rays. You and I can both trace our roots to the Second Ray. For this reason, we share a love of teaching. We will harmonize best with other teachers and artists, but interaction with other rays can provide rapid spiritual growth. An inherent friction exists between Fourth-Ray artists like your mother and Fifth-Ray engineers like your father, for example. But these differences also afforded them the opportunity to make great spiritual gains.

"You've heard of 'cat people' and 'dog people'? Those who gravitate to cats generally have a Fourth Ray in their makeup. While cats are Fourth-Ray animals, dogs draw their loyal characteristics from the Sixth Ray of Devotion.

"Spiritual masters choose beforehand which rays they will need to fulfill a particular mission here on Earth. Yagonquin, an ageless Tibetan lama, radiates great power. He draws his strength from the First Ray. One can surmise by his sense of order that he has a Seventh Ray in his makeup, perhaps in his causal body. Next to the personality ray, the causal ray plays the biggest role in our life here at present.

"I saw Yagonquin once while in India at the ashram. He had come to see the Great Master about business that didn't involve us students." The Chief glanced over with a hint of a smile. "But I did manage to pass within a few feet of him when he dined with us," he said. "The man radiated a powerful energy that was a heavy pulsation.

"Several years later I met Yagonquin on a street corner in Venice Beach, California. I was out for a late night walk, around midnight. As I neared a corner, I noticed a solidly built man holding two large, white garbage bags. I couldn't get a good look at him since he was wearing a tan poncho, the hood pulled up close around his face. Probably a homeless person, I thought, as I continued walking in the direction of the beach. About half a mile later I came to a dark industrial area and turned around.

"Retracing my steps, I found the man waiting on the same corner. I was a bit uneasy, so I planned a wide route around him. Then I heard a familiar voice inside my head. It was the Great Master. 'Speak to this man,' he urged.

"I stopped a few feet behind him, feeling even more nervous now, and tried to think of something intelligent to say. As I stood there staring up at the stars, the man yelled something indiscernible out loud at the top of his voice. It scared me so badly that I nearly bolted for my motel!

"I was shocked to find the Tibetan master standing before me in California. His guise as a beggar made the encounter even more bizarre. To this day, I can only remember parts of our conversation. The Great Master must have set up the meeting to teach me about power, however, for that seemed to be the primary theme. Yagonquin spoke about the three-fold flame, and the invincibility of the Inner Warrior.

"He said that within the heart of every person burns a three-fold flame of love, wisdom, and power. These three flames are actually currents of energy surrounding a perfect likeness of ourselves in the Temple of the Heart. This is our individual drop of God Consciousness from the Unchanging Ocean of Ecstasy, tailored to fit each embodiment. It's much easier to be humble when you realize that each person you meet is the god of his or her own universe.

"Yagonquin explained that the steel-blue flame within the heart is the source of our power. Our source of wisdom is the green flame; the current of love is a pinkish hue. By using the imagination, we can go to the Temple of the Heart and contact the three-fold flame. Little by little, we learn that we are not the bundle of fears and false judgments in our Belief System ruled by the ego.

"It takes an understanding of the Belief System, or 'Seedbed,' to become an Inner Warrior, he related. As we touched on earlier, this is an area in the subconscious mind, also called the reactive mind, where false judgments reside. These judgments daily shape our lives. We may have accepted the belief that we have to be perfect, for example. This is a tall order for anyone. Even worse, we may believe that we're 'born sinners.' These false beliefs limit our ability to give and receive love. They also destroy our self-esteem and undermine our personal power.

"The seeds of our karma are also stored in the Belief System. When we harm others, for example, we incur a debt to life. At a later time we will attract a similar experience in order to learn how it feels to be harmed. This is called the Law of Cause and Effect.

"An Inner Warrior has balanced these harmful thoughts within the Seedbed, either through physical experience or through contemplation. In other words, he has learned the lesson. He draws no harm to himself, and thereby becomes invincible. He radiates great power and self-confidence.

"Furthermore, an Inner Warrior doesn't feel guilty, for he understands that he can never wrong another. He knows there are no victims, only Souls attracting experiences they need for balancing negative thoughts stored in their Seedbed. For the same reason, an Inner Warrior doesn't think in terms of forgiveness. Forgiveness is based on the false assumption that one has been wronged. But forgiveness can be useful in releasing trapped emotions from the past, ones created during times of wrongful thinking.

"Not long after my meeting with Yagonquin," explained the Chief, "I set to work restoring my self-esteem by cleaning up my Belief System. I discovered that I had a lot of 'unlearning' to do."

I thanked the Chief for sharing these stories about his teachers with me. I told him that if I ever decided to clean out my Belief System I would have to rent a bulldozer!

According to the Chief, Horse Heaven was less than three miles away as the crow flies. His spirits were high as we crossed the mossy terrain in long strides. I could only imagine what he was feeling, returning to the sacred valley he had once called home so long ago. I could only wonder what he would find there, and what would eventually become of him. I doubted that I would ever see him again. In another week summer baseball would be under way, and my social life would no doubt take an upswing. Also, with college tuition due in three months, a summer job was a necessary distraction.

All in all, I looked upon the significance of my meeting with John Redstone with as much complacency as most teenagers. It would be a long time before I'd learn the priceless lesson of appreciation, and finally realize what a great blessing God had bestowed upon me.

The Summit of Wisdom

A badger fulfilled a life-long dream as he ascended the last fifteen yards of a steep mountain that towered high above the place of his birth. All his life he had prepared for this journey, boasting all the while of the great knowledge he would attain when at last he stood upon the summit of wisdom.

Wearily, but with great satisfaction, he slumped to the ground beneath a laurel tree to catch his breath. He could scarcely believe it. He was now the wisest badger in the entire forest! Proudly he rose, gazing out for the first time upon his expanded horizon. But as he did, his mouth fell open in disbelief.

What was this? Another mountain range beyond the one he stood upon, and another beyond that, and another, and another. Each one, it seemed, rose higher than the last. The badger felt very small indeed as he returned to the valley floor where an expectant crowd had assembled to greet him.

"What was it like?" they asked excitedly. "What awaits us at the summit of wisdom?"

"Hm...," the badger muttered, stumbling off into the forest. "Hm...I know nothing...Hmm."

The multitude fell silent. Looks of confusion passed among the crowd. "Whaat? What did he say?" they asked in bewilderment. "What lies at the summit?"

An elderly badger, one who'd grown deaf with the passing years, shouted out joyfully. *"Humility,"* he reported. "He said humility awaits us at the summit of wisdom."

A Very Small Door

A bear discovered a small door near the back of his cave. Being much too big to squeeze through, he called for the sleek mountain lion. Soon, a large crowd had gathered.

"If there is something fearful on the other side," explained the bear, "the mountain lion will be able to contend with it." But the door was too low for the mountain lion to crawl through.

"Summon the falcon," ordered the bear. "He is wise. If he makes it through, he can report back accurately on what he has found." But the falcon was also too big. Even the compassionate muskrat with his small stature was unable to slide through.

"It must be a door to heaven," speculated the eagle. "If that's the case, only someone with a very small ego can squeeze through. I'll bet a field mouse could do it."

The field mice stood about in a group, noticeably pleased that they were the only ones going to heaven. At last, one of the mice stepped forward. But as he approached the door his smile dimmed.

"What is it?" questioned his friends, as the silence became unbearable.

The tiny mouse lowered his head. "It is indeed a very small door," he called back anxiously.

The Most Humble Man

A stranger once stopped in the forest to camp. News of his humility spread quickly among the animals. "He's the most humble man I've ever seen," observed the eagle.

"And he carries himself with an uncommon dignity," spoke the bear, "not unlike the prophets of old."

In the shadows, the wolves laughed among themselves. "Yes, we've seen him," snickered one. "But he is not humble. He is a simple manure gatherer!" Thus saying, the wolves howled with ridicule.

One day the wolf that had spoken became seriously ill. His howls of ridicule turned to howls of pain. A healer was called, one new to the area. His secret roots and herbs brought miracles, some claimed. To the surprise of the wolves, the manure gatherer showed up at their door.

"I am the healer you sent for," announced the stranger, introducing himself. "I've picked up this bundle of manure for your fire."

The wolves watched in silence as the man mixed a potion and gave it to their sick brother. Within an hour he was gingerly moving about.

"You are indeed a great healer," proclaimed the grateful wolf. "Why bother yourself with the gathering of manure?"

"Our secrets," explained the man, "are handed down from father to son. They are ancient and powerful. The day I left home my father gave me this advice: 'Wherever you go and whomever you visit,' he told me, 'stop along the way and gather manure for their fire. Then you will never forget, my son, that humility is the soil from which our miracles grow.'"

Confessions of a Magpie

In the *Year of the Dancing Winds,* a magpie came home from his travels around the world. "I've returned to the woods," he reported, "not to live a good life, but to live life, whether it be good or bad."

Everyone marveled at his wisdom, unaware that Henry David Thoreau had made a similar statement long before.[14] Soon, the magpie became a speaker in great demand, with admirers as far north as Bristol Prairie. Life was to be experienced, he proclaimed, both the good and the bad. To learn from a mistake made the mistake worthwhile, for Soul is not tainted, no more than the sun can be tainted by the shadow of an oak.

The magpie lived a long life and became famous for his lectures on self-forgiveness and the value of living life to its fullest. Before he died, however, he wrote a full confession explaining that his life-work had been built on the foundation of a stolen truth.

He was forgiven by all, of course, and "The Confession" became known as a great piece of literature. But its author could never forgive the one who needed it most. He went to his grave thinking of himself only as a thieving magpie, for he could never escape the shadow of his own mistake.

Cottage Lights

One crisp winter night the prophet sat atop a grassy hill overlooking a purple lake and the cottages surrounding it. A blazing planet beamed low on the horizon. Nearby, the river of stars that was the Milky Way rippled its way through time and space. The sky was alive with a billion stars, radiating their beauty for all to see; yet only this single Soul gazed out upon the breathtaking spectacle with appreciation.

Below him lay the cottages in sleepy contentment. The prophet marveled at the scene before him. Because those living in the cottages could see this sight every night, perhaps they never would!

Back to Horse Heaven

You were once a proud pony
   with a thousand beside you,
as free as the grasses
   of Horse Heaven's plains.
Then they came with their ropes
   from the valley and tied you,
and led your free spirit
   from Horse Heaven's plains.

Now you learn about life
   from a whip and a harness,
enduring and learning
   the tug of the reins.
But you learned how to serve,
   and you learn how to give,
and you're better for living
   the hardship and pain.

With courage you rise
   when the burden is greatest.
You earn self-respect
   and a laborer's praise,
for you'll carry your share
   and a bit of another's.
You're still a proud pony
   from Horse Heaven's plains.

Then they learn you can run
   like none other before you,
with heels born of freedom
   on Horse Heaven's plains.

From a thousand you rise
  to the challenge before you,
and earn the respect
  due a champion's name.

So you learn about life
  on a track made of cinders,
enduring and learning
  the spoils of the game.
You learn to compete
  for the glamour of winning,
and you're better for living
  the glory and fame.

Then proudly you're led
  from the crowds and the spotlight
to evergreen meadows
  and clear placid streams,
where at last with the weight
  of a lifetime before you,
you're drawn to the light
  of an opening door.

And soon you are running
  through fields without fences,
back to Horse Heaven
  and Horse Heaven's plains.
Oh, soon you are running
  with a thousand proud ponies,
as free as the grasses
  of Horse Heaven's plains.

Chapter Eight
Freedom

Invisible Horses
CONVERSATION ON THE GRASSY KNOLL

When I remember the Chief, I see him sitting cross-legged on the grassy knoll overlooking Horse Heaven, his arms stretched skyward. I know now that returning home must have been a sad, sweet experience for him. The journey was the fulfillment of a simple dream; yet, more than that, it was the completion of a major cycle. As he had said, all things change whether we want them to or not.

We were greeted by a golden eagle sitting regally on a barbed-wire fence post like a wary sentinel. He showed little interest in the social antics of a flock of blackbirds as they dove in and out of the rushes flanking the creek. I noticed a couple of Guernsey cows milling around, but saw no horses.

Like the eagle, the Chief was a solitary character in this world. His old friends had either moved away or passed on. And even the silver thread that tied him to this world would soon be broken, I suspected. But he appeared happy, at least on the surface, and an unmistakable tone of contentment in his voice seemed to confirm this.

"Thomas Wolf once said, 'You can't go home,'" remarked the Chief. "But I have a feeling that it's impossible not to. It's a cycle. Like the salmon, the instinct is here within us." He touched a forefinger to his heart.

"All things begin in the heart," he said, "and in time, all things return to the heart. It's the center of our own universe. This is what the world's great myths are trying to tell us. The heart is the treasure.

"The saints talk about the great cycles, the entering into matter to experience ideas in motion, then the return to Divine Unity. These are the great cycles of myth. But there are also lesser cycles that span lifetimes. All cycles have a beginning and ending, but also a mid-point, beyond which there is no returning without the treasure. As Christ put it, 'There is no turning back once you put your hands to the plowshare handle.'"

The Chief fell silent and closed his eyes. Soon he was breathing deeply, as if to drink in the simple pleasures he had hidden away in the cattails along the creek as a boy. For several minutes he softly sang HU, the secret name of God, then went into the Silence.

After half an hour he suddenly thrust his arms toward the sky, breaking into a lengthy chant, or native song. When at last he opened his eyes, I asked him about his contemplation. He didn't speak immediately, and I got the impression that much of it was too personal to share. He did tell me, however, that the chant had been his song of freedom.

"I knew they'd be waiting for me," he finally mused. "The ponies are gone, but their spirits are still here running free. They were with me in the Silence," he confided with a smile.

"Horse Heaven has a name, a secret name. The ponies told me. It's called a *Place of Freedom*. They asked me to remember what it was like to be completely free. They asked me to imagine myself as the little boy who used to hide in the tall grass beside the creek, then chase them up into the mountains." The Chief smiled remembering his game.

"We're like the shadow people in Plato's cave," he related.[15] "Plato once wrote a story about a group of people living in a dark cave. They could not turn their heads because they were heavily chained. There was a fire behind them. All they could see were their shadows on the wall of the cave. Their only entertainment came from the shadow games they played. In time, they forgot they were people. They fell under the illusion that they were simply shadows on a wall.

"As the story goes, one day a prisoner broke free and found his way to the surface. The sunlit new world was a heaven to him, with its vibrant colors and blissful freedom. Being a compassionate Soul, the man went back into the dark cave to tell his friends about the higher world, and to inform them of the great spell they were under.

"But no one believed him. To make matters worse, the sunlight had blinded him. He couldn't see in the dark cave. His friends thought him a madman because he could no longer play the shadow games on the wall.

"A man needs to live on the edge a little, even if society disapproves." The Chief smiled. "Without a little madness it is difficult to break the chains and be completely free.

"You see, Michael, long ago our spirit was free. But then we pretended that we were limited beings so we could experience the passion and diversity that comes from living in physical bodies. As time went by, we forgot we were pretending. We began to believe we were the bodies we had manifested. We forgot the secret pathway back, the pathway of the imagination. This is what the ponies told me.

"They said I had passed the 'Test of Remembrance.' It was time for my return. It was time for me to follow Horseheaven Creek into the mountains, to return my treasure to God.

"It took many long seasons of clearing false judgments before it was possible to remember once again that *I AM*. Everything attached to I AM is by nature a limitation, a judgment of some kind, either good or bad. We must cease to identify with everything but love, or God, since God is love. Lastly, we must claim our freedom.

"To return to the awareness of I AM is to return to the eternal moment, beyond the illusion of time, where all peace, love, joy, bliss, happiness, and freedom await us. This is what the ponies told me."

Just then, the eagle gave a sharp cry and lifted off the fence post. I remembered the golden eagle in the Chief's dream about Eagle Rock, how it had symbolized the Great Spirit calling him home. At that very moment the Chief rose to his feet. Shielding his eyes from the sun, he traced the bird's flight up Horseheaven Creek. It was a powerful coincidence.

"I've enjoyed your company, my old friend," the Chief said warmly, turning to face me. He extended his hand. "An exciting life awaits you, Michael. I'm certain your quest for the Golden Heart will be a great success." He gathered up his few things and started down the slope toward the meadow. A stiff breeze was now rippling through the tall grass by the creek.

"What makes you so sure?" I called after him.

The Chief stopped, then wheeled about with a broad smile. Pointing toward Horse Heaven he called back, "The ponies told me!"

Wildflowers and Waterfalls

Fifty blackbirds, flying wingtip to wingtip, soared in formation through the mist above a pristine waterfall. They dove as one toward an emerald pool below the falls, admiring the beauty of the buttercups surrounding it.

High above them an eagle glided gracefully upon a powerful current of air, captivated by the breathtaking falls. Noticing the blackbirds below him, the eagle said to himself, "My pleasure is fifty times greater than theirs, for I don't have to share the experience with forty-nine others."

As a shadow fell across the face of the pool, the blackbirds looked up in unison at the solitary eagle. "His pleasure," they observed, "is only a fiftieth of ours. What a pity he has no one to share the experience with, thus multiplying his pleasure."

Living on the Edge

A woodpecker moved into a dead snag that had been hit twice by lightning. A young rabbit called up to him from the ground. "Why tempt fate?" he asked. "Wouldn't a life of moderation be a much safer life?"

"Anything worth doing," responded the woodpecker dramatically, "is worth doing to excess. It is only when we live on the edge of danger that we truly feel alive."

A few months later the rabbit met the woodpecker on a mountain trail. The bird's feathers had been singed, and he was badly shaken. "I'm moving to the mountains," stated the woodpecker, "to live a life of moderation. For only with moderation can we live a long life." Thus saying, he moved deep into the mountains and lived a very long life.

But as the rabbit observed at the funeral, while the life of the woodpecker had indeed been full, it had been excessively moderate.

The Dangerous Man

Panic swept through the Enchanted Forest when it was learned that a dangerous man was passing through. A group of frightened rabbits met with the prophet. "What shall we do?" they cried. "We must protect ourselves from this outcast of society."

The prophet questioned them further. "What has this man done to warrant such fear?"

"He believes not as society," answered a rabbit. "He laughs at the threat of burning for eternity."

"Not even death does he fear," stated another. "Nor does he work in the factories," added a third. "We've heard that he gets by without the comforts society offers."

At last the prophet understood. "Society fears this man," he explained, "for he is beyond its control. But I tell you this: The stars tremble in admiration when a free man passes."

On the Threshold of Freedom

A solitary eagle soared silently above a frozen waterfall. Below him, fifty blackbirds danced wingtip to wingtip between snow-laden firs and half-buried cabins.

Said the eagle, "What freedom can they enjoy in the shadow of forty-nine others?" Thus saying, he cried the secret cry of eagles and shot through the heavens on a course for the sun.

The blackbirds followed him with their eyes until he was lost from sight. "What little security an eagle enjoys," they observed, shaking their heads. "Even though he flies with the sun, he can never escape the shadow of solitude." Thus saying, they lit side by side on a telephone line and sang to the wind: "Fifty blackbirds are we/Fifty brothers of the wing/We fly as one."

But only forty-nine voices could be heard, for one bird's eyes were cast heavenward in admiration. Freedom comes on silent wings, and none can resist its burning call.

Wings Upon the Wind

Were you there among the shadows
    on some distant world away,
when the stars hid in their heavens,
    when the night winds brought the rain?

Did you come to light the darkness?
    Was it you I stood beside?
I can feel your strength enfold me.
    I can feel your hand in mine.

When my voice began to tremble
    all the others turned away.
Did you hear my spirit calling?
    Was it love that made you stay?

From your vision came my insight;
    from your wings my will to fly.
I can feel your blood course through me
    as our lifelines intertwine.

Was it fate that led you onward?
    Did you choose your time to go?
Could you feel your faith uplift me
    as I soared upon my own?
How your knowledge of survival
    eased the fear that made me cry.
Above the roaring of the tempest
    did I hear you say goodbye?

I can almost hear your laughter
    through the emptiness of time.
Your friendship lit my pathway;
    was it love that made it bright?

Did the eagles fly before you
    on your journey to the heights?
I can almost trace your footsteps
    in the patterns of their flight.[16]

Chapter Nine
The Quest

The Golden Heart
A Promise Kept at Watson Falls

When I unpacked my camping gear that night in the Watson Falls parking lot where I was to meet my mom the next day, I discovered the Chief's dream catcher. I'd seen how carefully he'd handled the fragile ring of feathers his grandfather had given him so many years before. Even at that age, I understood the significance of the gift.

From some deeper part of myself I felt tears welling up from an ancient spring. I didn't try to hold them back. Sitting there holding the dream catcher below the waterfall in the red-orange afterglow of the day, I realized for the first time that I'd been through a life-changing experience.

That summer I played some of the best baseball of my life, despite long hours spent behind a dryer in a plywood mill earning money for school. In September I started college as planned, studying Western Civilization and Business, as well as English. A class on religion was also required.

By Christmas I was painfully aware of how unsatisfying a social education is to the Soul. I felt more and more out of place in that environment. From time to time I thought about the

Chief, remembering how much at home I'd felt around him and his ideas. I wondered what had become of him. And I wondered what would become of me.

On the morning of December 26th I drove up to Colliding Rivers and sat in my car for over an hour thinking about the future. It was Christmas vacation, but only a handful of tourists stopped to read the plaque on their way to Crater Lake. Should I return to school, I wondered, or ask for my old job back at the plywood mill? I kept hoping the Chief would suddenly appear and help me decide.

That night I stayed up late thinking about the Chief's discourses and stories, jotting down notes to help remember them later. Sometime after midnight I fell asleep on the couch in front of a comfortable fire. Once again I found myself dreaming about Colliding Rivers.

I was an old man in the dream, even older than the Chief. I'd brought my grandson to Colliding Rivers to celebrate his eighth birthday. The two of us were fishing from the Little River side. A narrow footpath led through a grove of tall firs behind us, following the river. A Great Blue Heron fished in the shallow water not fifty yards upstream, seemingly oblivious to our presence.

"Tell me a story, Grandfather," my grandson urged in the dream. He put down his pole and gathered a handful of rocks. "Tell me again why Great Blue Heron is the greatest of all birds."

"Well," I began, tying some new line to the crude pole, "many long seasons ago a wealthy white trader came over the Cascade Range." I pointed to the east. "You see, he'd heard stories about Great Blue Heron. He'd heard that Heron possessed the most valuable object in the Land of the Umpquas.

"The man knew little about spiritual things, and was only interested in wealth. He vowed he would have Heron's treasure at any price." The young Indian boy threw his last rock. After wiping both hands on his deerskin pants, he picked up his pole and gave me his full attention.

"When the man tracked Heron down," I continued, "he got a big surprise. You see, Heron was only a very poor bird. But even though he was poor, he was very kind and very wise.

"Heron said sadly, 'I've found that people don't own possessions — their possessions own them. It is true, however,' he continued, 'I do own this object. But as you can see, I do not own it. Therefore, it is not mine to sell.' The confused man became very angry.

"'And why not?' he demanded.

"'Let me tell you a story,' Heron said. 'Something happened long ago during a terrible storm. One dark and rainy night a tired fisherman stopped here seeking shelter. With my outstretched wings I kept his bed dry. He was very grateful. To show his appreciation, he gave me his most-prized possession. It was a heart of gold.' The man's eyes lit up with greed as he estimated the value of the Golden Heart.

"'In reality,' replied Heron, 'it was only a gold-colored shell. But it was worn in such a way that it resembled a heart. This stranger said to me, "To possess this heart is not to possess it, for the holder of the heart is the giver of life. One may only possess it who gives it away. From hand to hand, from heart to heart, throughout eternity it must freely pass.'

"'Upon saying this,' Heron said, 'he gave me the heart and disappeared into the mountains above Horse Heaven. When the time was right, I gave it to another, who in turn, I assume, gave it to someone else.

"'I would gladly give you what you seek,' replied Heron sympathetically, but only God knows the holder of the Golden Heart.'"

"That was good, Grandfather," the boy responded enthusiastically. "Do you think I could learn to talk to the animals?"

"Belief is a powerful thing," I answered, savoring the moment. "Yes! I believe it is possible," I finally said. "What about you? What do you believe?"

"I don't know," he answered thoughtfully, grabbing another fistful of rocks. "But if I ever learn how, I'll ask Heron to help me find the Golden Heart."

"That reminds me," I said, reaching into my leather pack. "I have something for you. Maybe it will help you on your quest for the Golden Heart."

His eyes sparkled as I handed him the gift. "Thank you, Grandfather," he exclaimed, examining the hoop with the seven colored eagle feathers. "I'll always treasure it...*and when I find the Golden Heart, I'll give this back so you can find it too!*"

"That would be nice, Young Heron," I said with a hearty laugh. "We'd better head for home. We've got a long walk ahead of us."

Suddenly, the Great Blue Heron took to the air with a startled cry. He made a sweeping circle above the mist, then passed overhead with his wings fully extended as if to imitate the bird in the story.

"How did you know I wanted a dream catcher for my birthday, Grandfather?" the boy asked.

I gathered up our fishing poles and pointed to the bird, who had now resumed fishing at his favorite pool.

"Heron told me." I answered with a wink.

Shadows of a Fisherman

An old man caught a fish where the rivers collide,
then he moved to the mountains to examine his life.
And there in the solitude he realized with a thrill
that he was the poet who'd gone to the woods,
that he was the healer who had gathered manure,
and the eagle, the blackbirds,
the field mice, and the forest,
for all were the shadows of his own ideas;
their weaknesses his; their strengths his own.
Now he plays with the children
and he runs with the wolves
near the bridge that was built
for the fishermen that follow.

*   *   *

Few people fish where the rivers collide on Highway 138 near Glide, Oregon, for no one can be sure whether the wind from the gorge carries the laughter of children or the howling of wolves.

NOTES

<u>Map of the Enchanted Forest</u>

1. For those interested in visiting the Colliding Rivers area in southern Oregon, consider stopping by the Colliding Rivers Information Center for a copy of "Thundering Waters," a complimentary brochure featuring maps and pictures of waterfalls in the Umpqua National Forest: 18782 N. Umpqua Hwy., Glide, Oregon 97443, (541) 496-0157.

   NOTE: The Chief's "Enchanted Forest" varies slightly from the actual area.

<u>Author's Note</u>

2. For more details on these initial conversations, as well as additional topics, please see *Touched by the Dragon's Breath: Conversations at Colliding Rivers* (Susan Creek Books, 2005). This book is thoroughly indexed for readers' convenience.

<u>Chapter 1: Truth</u>

3. Reference to the *Nezic* can be found on a display at the Colliding Rivers Viewpoint.

4. Umpqua means "Thundering Water" (Thundering Waters brochure).

<u>Chapter 2: Wisdom</u>

5. Hazrat Khan wrote: "In reality wisdom is love and love is wisdom, although in one person wisdom may be predominant and in another love."

   "The spiritual Message of Hazrat Inayat Khan,"

Volume VIIIa (Sufi Teachings), Part IV (Love) on http.wahiduddin.net/mv2/VIIIa/VIIIa_4_1.

6. Two versions of the "HU Song" CD and tape are available through ECKANKAR: www.eckankar.org, 1-800-LoveGod.

Chapter 3: Love

7. Inspired by "The Bridge Builder," a poem written by Will Allen Dromgoole, circa 1900. www.storybin.com/builders/builders165.shtml

Chapter 4: Tolerance

8. A mural of the Wheel of Life, similar to the one described by the Chief in his dream, appears on the cover of *The ECK-Vidya: Ancient Science of Prophecy,* by Paul Twitchell (Illuminated Way Press, 1972). The *ECK-Vidya* is an excellent resource for further exploration into the twelve sections (nidanas) of the Wheel of Life.

Chapter 5: Discrimination

9. See *The Secret Language of Waking Dreams,* by Michael Avery (ECKANKAR, 1992).

10. Adapted from the story "Creatures of Habit," *The Secret Language of Waking Dreams,* pp. 16-17.

11. Inspired by an unpublished poem by Jamie Davis, "Moments Hurry By."

Chapter 7: Humility

12. Daryai Lal Kapur, *Call of the Great Master* (Radha Soami Satsang Beas, Fifth Edition, 1978) p. xxix. The quote reads: "Every one, whether man, woman or child, said the Great

Master loved him most."

13. For more information on the Seven Rays, see *A Treatise on the Seven Rays, Volume 2: Esoteric Psychology, Vol. II.,* by Alice Bailey and Djwal Khul (Lucis Trust, 1942).

    NOTE: 7 Rays X 12 nidanas (of the Wheel of Life) = 84 major life experiences.

14. Henry David Thoreau wrote in "Civil Disobedience," his 1849 essay: "I came into this world not chiefly to make this a good place to live in, but to live in it, be it good or bad." Carl Bode, *The Portable Thoreau* (Penguin Books, 1947) p. 120.

Chapter 8: Freedom

15. The Allegory of the cave was used by Plato in *The Republic.* It was told and then interpreted by Socrates at the beginning of Book 7, pp. 514a–520a. (The Colonial Press, 1901, translated by Benjamin Jowett.)

16. "Wings Upon the Wind" is dedicated to Mr. Redstone, the Chief.

TOUCHED by the
DRAGON'S BREATH
Conversations at Colliding Rivers

Touched by the Dragon's Breath is based on actual conversations that took place between Michael Harrington and his mentor, John Redstone, splashed against the backdrop of Colliding Rivers in southern Oregon. These weekly discussions, spanning more than three years, explain in detail the significance of 2012, the Photon Belt, Zero Point, the light wave of creation, and the 50-year, Time/Space Overlap Zone between the Piscean Age and the Age of Aquarius.

In two related conversations about the Seedbed and the Mirror of Life, John Redstone reveals his step by step approach to cleaning up the Belief System, a key element in preparing for the global frequency shift—commonly called the "Shift of the Ages"—that will usher in a new Golden Age.

In a separate chapter highlighting prophecies from the Hopi, Maya, Aztec, and Tibetan cultures, the author substantiates many of Mr. Redstone's views on 2012 and the Photon Belt, a spectacular band of multi-dimensional light, secretly known to some as the "Dragon's Breath."

The author also provides valuable, little-known information about water, as well as personal glimpses into his own spiritual journey; most notably, a quest that began over 70,000 years ago in the ancient land of Lemuria.

ISBN#: 978-0-9748716-0-8   (228 pgs.)

ABOUT THE AUTHOR

Michael Harrington has been interested in spiritual subjects for over 30 years. His fascination with metaphysics began at the age of fourteen, when he was taken by a spiritual adept on an out-of-the-body journey to a Temple of Wisdom similar to the one described by the Chief in this book.

Trained as a water quality specialist, Michael began his working life in the plywood mills of Oregon. After finishing college, he worked briefly as a real estate developer with his brother, before striking out on his own to pursue writing.

Michael's first success came in the early '80's when one of his children's books, *The Catbird's Secret,* was accepted by a large publisher. The project later fell through; but the experience yielded sufficient motivation to continue writing. In 1990 he wrote *The Secret Language of Waking Dreams,* a popular book on synchronicity (published under a different name in 1992).

In 2005 Michael founded Susan Creek Books, named for a famous stream near Colliding Rivers in southern Oregon. *Touched by the Dragon's Breath* came out that same year, followed by this book, *Porcupines at the Dance* (2008). A third book in the Colliding Rivers series, *Wide Awake in Dreamland: Reflections from Colliding Rivers,* will feature the author's final conversations with Mr. Redstone, an update on 2012, and the "Tao of Sat Shatoiya."